WINDOWS 11
FOR SENIORS

The Most Complete Easy-to-Follow Guide to Master Your New PC. Unlock All Its Features with Step-by-Step Illustrated Instructions and Useful Tips and Tricks

Gary Watts

Table of Contents

Introduction

Glossary

Application: The code installed into your computer that performs specific tasks or functions. They are also known as programs or software.

Browser: An application used to access and navigate the internet, such as Google Chrome, Microsoft Edge, or Firefox.

CPU: "Central Processing Unit," the unit that works as the 'brain' of the computer, carrying out arithmetic and logic calculations.

Crash: This is when a piece of software or hardware malfunctions.

Cursor: The arrow on the screen connected to your mouse designed to carry out actions by clicking.

Default: The settings or programs that come standard with your computer.

Desktop: The main directory or working area of your computer used to access other directories and applications.

Disk: The storage device installed into your computer.

Download: the process of transferring data, such as programs, photos, files and documents, or other media, from the internet into your computer.

Email: "Electronic mail," a digital message that can be sent using the internet.

Hardware: The physical and mechanical components that are installed into your computer such as hard drives, chips, keyboards, monitors, etc.

Icons These are pictures that represent links to a program or function on your computer.

Input device: The hardware you use to interact with your computer, such as a mouse, keyboard, microphone, etc.

Install: The act of preparing and making software or hardware ready for use.

Interface: A device like a monitor or a program like a desktop that enables you to communicate with your computer.

Internet: Interconnected computer networks.

Memory: Information stored on your computer.

Menu: A list of options that can carry out different functions. It can include pop-up menus, drop-down menus, and more.

Monitor: The screen or visual display connected to your computer.

Mouse: Hardware that you move about with your hand to control the on-screen cursor and click buttons.

MP3: A file format used to store video and audio data.

Multimedia: Any kind of media, including audio and video.

Network: A system of interconnected computers.

Operating system: Software that manages all other software and hardware on your computer, laptop, or tablet, ensuring that all files, programs, and processes can access the hard drives, processing units, memory, and storage efficiently and adequately.

Plug and play: Hardware that can be plugged in and is instantly recognized by the computer, allowing them to be used right away, like a mouse, keyboard, hard drive, etc.

Program: Same as application.

RAM: 'Random Access Memory' is stored in your computer used to help run background processes for different programs, helping them run faster.

Virus: A code that can copy itself and cause damage to your computer or threaten your computer security. Malware is similar.

Webcam: A digital camera that connects to your computer and can send live footage to the internet.

Window: A section of your display that is used to show the graphics of a program.

Word processor: A program used to create, edit, and save documents.

What Is Windows 11

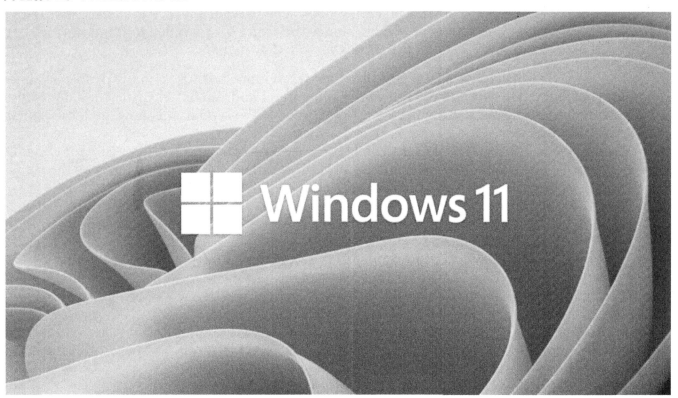

Windows 11 is the latest version of Microsoft's Windows operating system. An operating system manages all software and hardware on your computer, laptop, or tablet, ensuring that all files, programs, and processes can access the hard drives, processing units, memory, and storage efficiently and adequately.

There have been several different versions of Windows released over the years. Windows 1 was released in 1985, evolving into more modern versions such as Windows 95, Windows XP, Windows

7, Windows 8, Windows 10, and the most recent version, which we will learn about in this book. Each version has seen updates and changes to how the operating system looks and feels and more technical changes that run in the background to make your experience with your computer more intuitive and efficient.

There are other operating systems that can run on computers, such as Linux, Ubuntu, Android, ChromeOS, and macOS. Each of these operating systems is designed to meet the specific needs of different users. Some are better for carrying out office tasks like writing documents and emails, while others write code and develop software. Operating systems are also designed for different kinds of devices; for example, smartphones use Android or IOS, which are made for mobile devices and suited for running small apps, whereas computers need more comprehensive operating systems with many different hardware and software.

Windows 11, like other operating systems, presents you with a graphical user interface. This allows you to communicate with your computer system, your mouse, or touchscreen by clicking on different symbols or icons. Before graphical user interfaces were the norm, character user interfaces were used. In a character user interface or command-line interface, you would have to write specific lines of code or commands to carry out different tasks and functions.

What Is New Windows Compared To Previous Version?

Windows 11 was designed around security and power. For it to run, it requires a special trusted platform module (TPM) chip. This special chip makes your PC more secure than ever, but then it comes at a price, as older PCs lack a TPM chip. Hence they can't be upgraded to Windows 11. There are some big changes that Windows 11 brings to your PC; they include:

•   **Taskbar.** This has to be the biggest difference in Windows 11 for so many people as all the icons are now centered on the taskbar as against being lined up from left to right. The Start button has also experienced migration from the lower-left corner of the screen; it is now the leftmost icon on the centered taskbar.
•   **Start menu.** This does no longer include those square icons which display constant updates on news, mails, weather and other information (live tiles) rather, the Start menu shows three rows of icons along its top half while saving its bottom half for frequently-used apps.
•   **Widgets:** With the elimination of live tiles from the Start Menu, Microsoft recreated the concept and made the Widgets panel. This is a strip of tiles designed to update and show the latest news, traffic information, photos and other information.
•   **Teams Chat:** In a bid to take advantage of the recent popularity of Zoom video chatting due to the pandemic, Microsoft built a program that aids video chatting in Windows 11. It is called Teams Chat and allows you to to hold video chats and exchange messages with friends, family and colleagues.
•   **Updates:** Windows 10 was treated as an ongoing service, and Microsoft released two huge updates each year. Thankfully, this wouldn't be the case with Windows 11, as Microsoft has pledged to update the new Windows just once a year.
•   **Apps:** There is usually an update of apps on Windows 11 daily or weekly, addition and elimination of new and unpopular features, respectively, and fixing problems. The updates can be found on the Microsoft Store App and they arrive automatically. With this, you're spared the hassle of searching for the latest updates. **Also, there' a bit of surprises;** apps may have a new outlook or appearance as also in their behavior from what they were the previous day.
•   **Stringent hardware requirements:** This means that you may not be able to upgrade your old Windows 10 PC; talk more of Windows 7 or Windows 8 PC to work with the new Windows 11.

- **Cortana.** The digital assistant from Windows 10 has been fully removed from Windows 11. If you never liked Cortana, this would be awesome news to you, but if not, you can simply click the Start button, type "Cortana" and just like usual, your biddings will be done.
- **No Tablet mode.** Windows 11 no longer has the Tablet mode, which made Windows behave differently on touch-screens. It rather looks and acts the same way on both desktops, PCs, laptops and tablets.

If your Windows PC is powerful enough to run Windows 11, it will probably get updated automatically through Windows Update in late 2021 or early 2022 but if reverse is the case, Windows 10 will keep running until October 2025. At that point, security patches will no longer be issued for Windows 10 and Microsoft will begin to nudge you to get a new PC.

Windows 11 Hardware Requirement

Hardware Requirement

To allow devices to install or upgrade to Windows 11, they must comply with the following minimum hardware specifications:

Processor: A processor with a clock speed of one gigahertz (GHz) or more and two or more cores in a compatible processor or 64-bit system-on-chip (SoC).

RAM: 4 gigabytes (GB) or more.

Memory: Installing Windows 11 requires 64GB* or more of available memory.

Additional storage space may be required to download updates and activate specific functions.

Video card: DirectX 12 or later compatible with WDDM 2.0 driver.

System software: UEFI, with secure boot support.

TPM: Trusted Platform Module (TPM) version 2.0.

Display: High Definition (720p) display, 9" or larger, 8 bit per color channel.

Internet connection: Updates and downloads and use of some features are available only with an Internet connection.

When using Windows 11 Home Edition for the first time, you will need an Internet connection and a Microsoft account to complete the device setup.

Over time, there may be additional requirements for updates and the inclusion of certain features in the operating system.

Requirements For The Operating System
Some Windows 11 features have extra requirements in addition to the ones already there. See the following list of features and the requirements for each one.

5G Compatibility: Requires 5G modem.

Auto HDR: An HDR display is required.

BitLocker to Go - Requires a USB flash drive. This feature is available on Windows Pro and above.

Cortana: Requires microphone and speaker and is currently available on Windows 11 for Australia, Brazil, Canada, China, France, Germany, India, Italy, Japan, Mexico, Spain, UK, and the US.

DirectStorage: NVMe SSD is required to store and run games using standard NVM Express Controller drivers and DirectX12 GPU with Shader Model 6.0 support.

DirectX 12 Ultimate: Available with compatible games and graphics chips.

Presence: This feature requires sensors that can determine a person's distance from the device and their intent to interact with the device.

Smart video conferencing: requires a video camera, microphone, and speakers (audio output)

Multiple voice assistants: microphone and speaker required.

Width: The 3-column layout requires an effective screen width of 1920 pixels or more.

Mute and unmute audio: The taskbar requires a video camera, microphone, and speakers (audio output). The app must support the global mute/unmute feature.

Space Audio: Additional hardware and software required.

Equipment required for Microsoft Teams includes a video camera, microphone, and audio speakers (audio output).

Touch: Touch requires a monitor or display capable of supporting multiple touches.

Two-factor authentication: Requires a PIN, biometrics (fingerprint reader or illuminated infrared camera), or Wi-Fi or Bluetooth-capable phone.

Voice input: Only computers with microphones can accept voice input.

Wake on Voice: Wake on Voice requires a modern standby source model and a microphone.

Wi-Fi 6E: Requires a new IHV WLAN controller and hardware and a Wi-Fi 6E compatible router/access point.

Windows Hello: Requires a camera configured to capture near-infrared (IR) images or a fingerprint scanner for biometric authentication.

Windows projection: Windows projection requires the use of a display adapter that supports Windows Display Driver Model (WDDM) 2.0 and a Wi-Fi adapter that supports the Wi-Fi Direct specification.

Xbox App: Xbox Live account required, not available in all regions.

The following configuration requirements apply to virtual machines running Windows 11.

Memory: 64 GB or more

- **Security:** Secure boot with virtual TPM support

Memory: 4 GB or more

- **Processor:** 2 or more virtual processors

The VM host CPU must also be able to meet the requirements of the Windows 11 CPU.

Note: The required virtual machine settings configuration procedure depends on the type of host that hosts the virtual machine. For host VMs running Hyper-V, virtualization (VT-x, VT-d) must be enabled in the BIOS. Virtual TPM 2.0 is emulated on the guest virtual machine, regardless the presence of TPM version of the Hyper-V host.

Features Of Windows 11

Android Apps

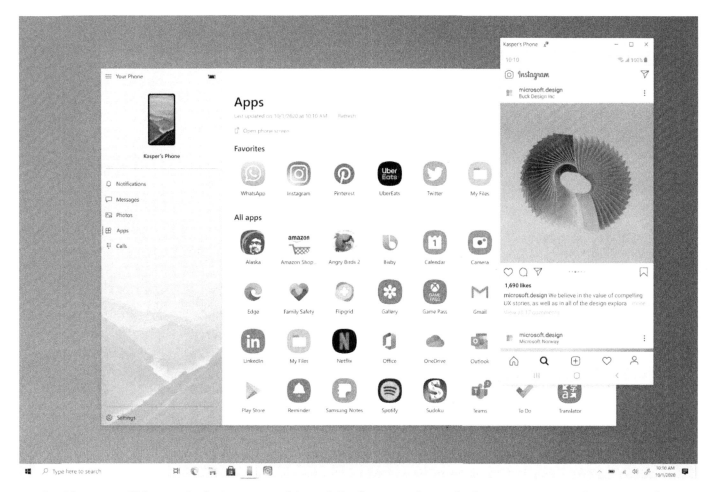

Android apps will be natively integrated into Windows 11 through the new Microsoft Store, a change Windows users have been expecting for years. Note, however, that support for Android apps was not part of the first shipping version of Windows 11.

How to use the Android app:

As soon as Windows 11 can handle them, Android apps will appear in the new Microsoft Store through the Amazon App Store. That means you must download the Amazon Appstore to access nearly 500,000 apps available, including Disney Plus, TikTok, Netflix, Pinterest, and Uber. However, you won't be able to access all the Android apps available in the Google Play Store.

The Amazon Appstore must be downloaded, and you must sign in or create an Amazon account before you can start using the service. Then you can search for free or paid apps like you would on any other platform. In addition to the start bar appearance, Android apps will also appear on the taskbar, each with its window.

Widgets

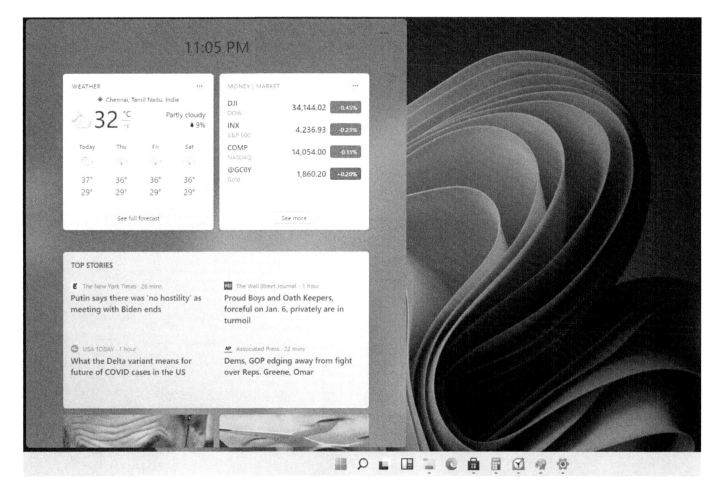

Windows 11 adds widgets to the interface, a customizable AI-powered slider to show you information like news, weather, a quick look at your calendar and to-do lists, and your recent photo. Widgets are comparable to "News and Interests" in the latest version of Windows 10.

How to use the Widget:

On the updated taskbar you will find a widget button. When you click or tap, a table appears on the left side of the screen with a series of widgets that give you a summary of the information you are looking for. You can also make it full screen by clicking on it.

Microsoft Team

Open the Microsoft Teams chat panel directly from the taskbar in Windows 11 for easy access to your contacts.

Windows 11 integrates the Microsoft Teams video chat platform directly into the operating system, making it easy to access for everyday use. You can chat with other Teams users on Windows, Android, Mac, or iOS.

How to use the Microsoft Team:

You can see Groups on the taskbar. If not, then you can search. Click the Groups icon to launch a chat tool that lets you choose to send a message, text, voice call, or video call to one of your contacts. Meet or chat with the person you want to chat with, or open the full version of Microsoft Teams by clicking the box at the bottom of the chat screen. To start a meeting, select Meet or chat with the person you want to chat with.

Desktop

Windows 11 makes it easy to create separate virtual desktops for every part of your life and customize them with different backgrounds so you can create one for personal, work use, school, game, or whatever and easily switch between them. This is similar to the virtual desktop feature in macOS.

How to use the Desktop:

Click the monitor button on the taskbar to open the panel with the current monitor. To create a new screen, click the plus button in the New Screen box. Press the X button to delete it. Then touch the screen to switch to it.

SHOOTING COMPOSITION

When you have multiple windows open and want to arrange them in a different layout on your desktop, Windows 11 allows you to do this, and all windows remain in their current location.

How to use Shooting Composition:

When you open the window, you will see a square button between the X and the minimize button in the upper right corner. Hover over it to see different layout options for that window, and select the layout and position in the layout where you want to place that window.

Bring groups of apps and windows together with a fixed layout, and easily get in and out of them with linked groups in Windows 11.

Snapshot Group
The group of active windows has been saved in Snapshot Layout and can be found on the taskbar for easy access to restore so they can be minimized or maximized as a group can be found in the Snapshot Group.

How to use Snapshot Group:

Step on your browser on the taskbar (it's unclear if you need to use Microsoft Edge to do this, as Microsoft did in its demo). You'll see the different groups of sites and apps you've created. To reopen the entire group, select the group you want and click it.

Chapter 1:
Installing Windows 11

Installing Via Windows Update

Before you can upgrade to Windows 11, ensure to check if your PC meets the minimum requirements. When you upgrade to Windows 11 it will keep all contents on your hard drive. However, make sure you have a backup before you initiate the upgrade process. And you could backup your files to OneDrive or an external drive.

Note that upgrading to Windows 11 is free.

- Go to the Start Menu or Action Center and select Settings or All Settings.
- Click the option **Update & Security**.

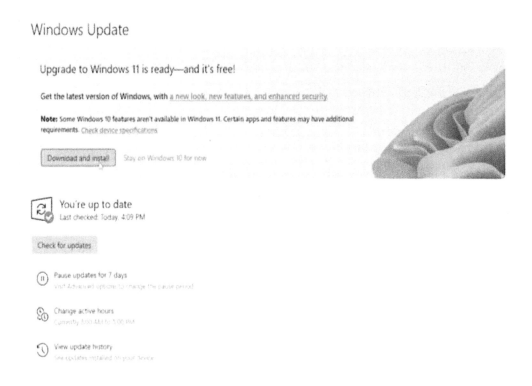

At the top of the display, you will notice if you can upgrade.

- Click the link, Download and install.
- On the Software License Terms screen, select the button Accept and install.

That is it, the process might take some time, but after its completion, your device will be running Windows 11 operating system.

Using The Installation Assistant To Install

A second way to install Windows 11 on your computer is via the Microsoft website. From the website, you can download the Windows 11 program and install it. You can use this method if you don't see the option to install Windows 11 on your computer settings' Update & Security tab.

To begin this process, ensure your computer is connected to the internet. Next, go to this link: https://www.microsoft.com/en-us/software-download

Doing so will lead you to a page that looks like this:

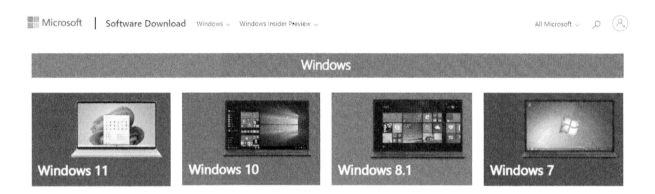

From the screenshot, you will see four different Windows versions available for download. The latest one is Windows 11, so click the option that says Windows 11 to proceed to the Windows 11 download page, as shown on the screenshot below.

Microsoft gives you three options for installing Windows 11 on your computer. Assuming that your computer is for personal use, you can select the first option. If your computer doesn't meet the minimum requirements for installing Windows 11 normally, click the dropdown of the third option and select Windows 11.

Click Download Now under the Windows 11 Installation Assistant option for normal installation. This will download the Windows 11 installer on your computer. By default, you will find it in the Download folder. Right-click the icon and select **Open**. The system will then ask whether you want to allow the program to make changes on your computer. Click **Yes**.

When you click Yes, the Windows 11 Installation Assistant page will open.

Windows 11 Installation Assistant

This is the best option for installing Windows 11 on the device you're currently using. Click **Download Now** to get started.

⊕ Before you begin

[Download Now]

Create Windows 11 Installation Media

If you want to perform a reinstall or clean install of Windows 11 on a new or used PC, use this option to download the media creation tool to make a bootable USB or DVD.

⊕ Before you begin

[Download Now]

Download Windows 11 Disk Image (ISO)

This option is for users that want to create a bootable installation media (USB flash drive, DVD) or create a virtual machine (ISO file) to install Windows 11. This download is a multi-edition ISO which uses your product key to unlock the correct edition.

Select Download ⌄

⊕ Before you begin

[Download]

 Windows 11 Installation Assistant   —

Use the PC Health Check app to check compatibility

To see if your device meets the system requirements to run Windows 11, use the PC Health Check app then come back here and select **Refresh**. Get PC Health Check app

Refresh	Close

■ Microsoft

In the screenshot, you will find a link that says "Get PC Health Check App." Click on this link to scan your system and ensure that your computer meets all the criteria for installing the Windows 11 software.

Once the health check has been completed, a message will appear informing you that your PC has met the requirements. If your PC doesn't meet the requirements, a corresponding notification will also appear.

Assuming the health check goes well, we can proceed to the next step. You will be required to agree with the terms of conditions of Microsoft. Agree to the terms to proceed to the next step. Just click on the succeeding **Next** buttons and the **Finish** button. Clicking the **Finish** button will prompt your computer to restart fully. The entire process will take some time, and your computer will turn off and on again several times. Your computer will also inform you how much of the installation process has been completed via a percentage bar. And once the installation has been completed, your computer will look like this:

How To Perform A Clean Installation With Windows 11

You can install a fresh or clean copy of Windows 11 if you don't want to upgrade to Windows 11 from your previous Windows. Installing a fresh copy of Windows 11 will utterly erase all the content on your hard drive and will in turn, install a clean Windows 11 operating system on your PC.

Microsoft features a PC health check tool that will let you know if your device can run Windows 11.

Go to **https://www.microsoft.com/en-us/windows/windows-11#pchealthcheck** and click the link **DOWNLOAD PC HEALTH CHECK APP.** And after installing the app, run it, and you will know whether your device can run Windows 11.

Because clean installation of Windows 11 will erase any content on your hard drive, therefore, ensure you back up some important files you want to keep. You can bring in an external hard drive to back up the files or opt for Microsoft OneDrive to sync files with the cloud.

The next thing is to get a product key. You can use the product key of Windows 7, 8, 10 or 11. All these product keys will work. To get a product key, click on the **Search** on the taskbar and enter the command prompt. Then select the best-matched option **Command Prompt App.** And type these commands on the **Command Prompt** interface- **wmic path softwarelicensingservice get OA3xOriginalProductKey** and tap Enter to view your Product key.

And if you don't have a license key, you can purchase one from Microsoft. Visit **https://www.microsoft.com/en-us/d/windows.**

And if you previously used the Windows operating system on the computer, re-installing Windows 11 with the same Microsoft account will automatically activate the operating system.

That said, it is time to create Windows 11 installation media. Visit https://www.microsoft.com/en-us/software and click on the link Download Now under the heading **Create Windows 11 Installation Media.** After downloading the file, go ahead to open the file.

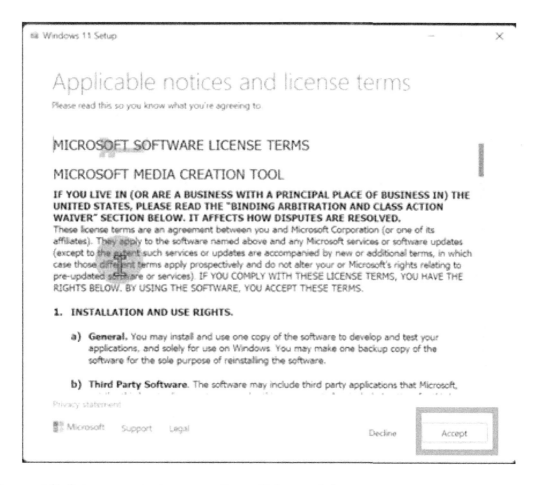

Click the **Accept** link to agree to terms and conditions of the app.

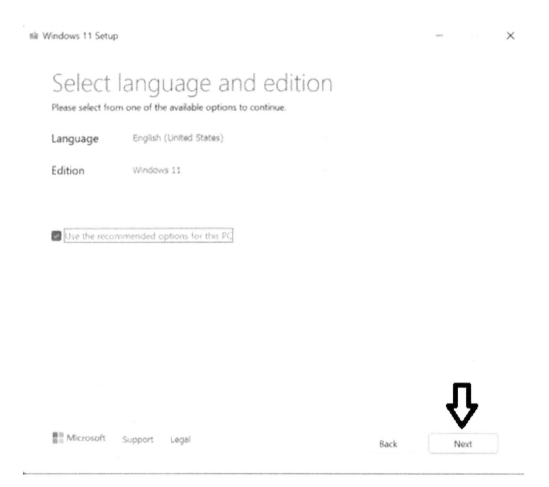

Select language and edition

Please select from one of the available options to continue.

Language   English (United States)

Edition   Windows 11

☑ Use the recommended options for this PC

Microsoft   Support   Legal   Back   Next

From the screen above, you can select your preferred language, choose the edition, or use the recommended settings. Click **Next** at the bottom right to proceed. Select where you want to create the installation media, and it is recommended to use a removable drive. And you need about 8GB of storage to install this operating system.

Restart your PC after creating media installation. And then boot the device from USB media. To do this, tap the **F2** or **ESC** keys to display various boot options.

On the Windows Setup screen, select **Next** to proceed with the installation process.

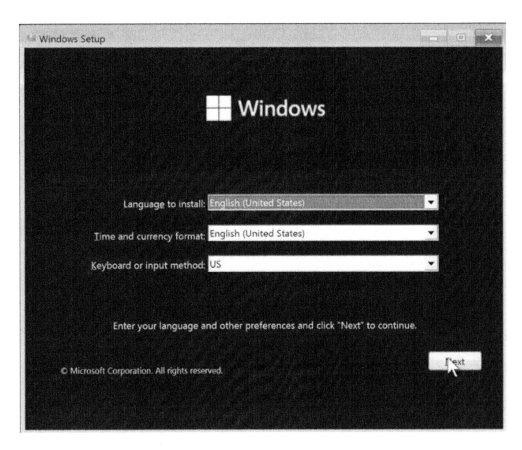

Click on **Install now** on the next screen. And if you want to do a clean installation, select the **Custom** option.

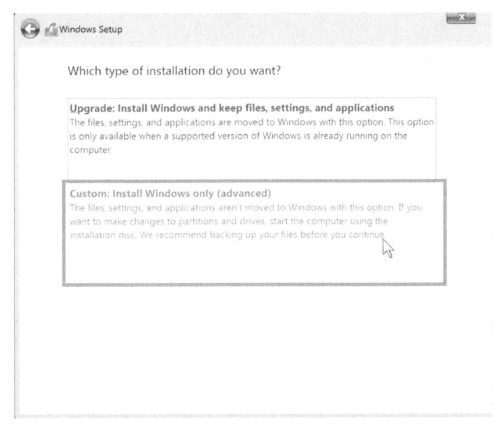

Then select the location on your PC where you desire to install the operating system. And take some time out to wait for the installation to start.

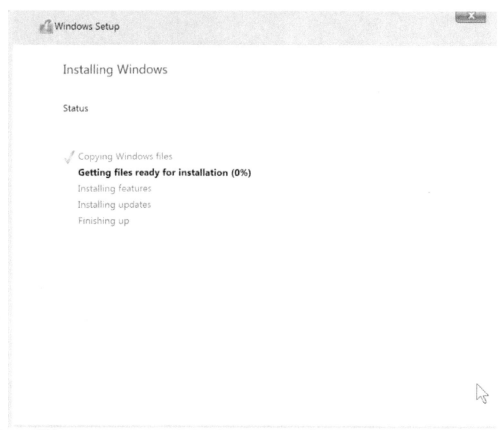

The installation will have to get to 100% for the process to be successful.

What You Should Know Before Installing Windows 11 On Non-Supported Devices

It can be annoying after downloading Windows 11 Operating System and on making an attempt to install it on your computer, get the message that reads, **"This PC doesn't currently meet Windows requirements"** as shown below:

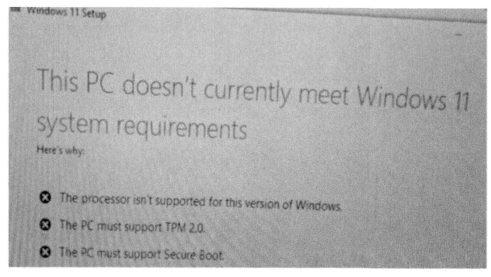

From the above notification, the issue is with the PC processor, PC does not support TPM 2.0, and PC does not support Secure Boot. But in some computers, the issues are usually with the TPM 2.0 and Secure Boot. Whether the issues are the three listed above or just two, I will guide you on how to fix it, and at the end, you will have Windows 11 up and running on your computer.

But make sure your PC has a minimum of 4 Gigabytes RAM, minimum of 64 Gigabytes disk space, and a display of 720P, and your computer must be running Windows 10 OS currently.

Installing Windows In An Unsupported Device

Don't panic if your PC does not meet the minimum hardware requirements to run Windows 11 or if the device has the minimum hardware requirements, but you did not get the **Download & Install** link on the **Update & Security** interface on your PC.'You can still run the operating system on your device.

Windows requires that your device has 8th generation or newer Intel processors, TPM 2.0 among others.

Any time you try to upgrade without meeting the minimum hardware requirements, you will get a response saying **This PC doesn't currently meet Windows 11 system requirements.**

To install Windows 11 on any unsupported device;

- Go to: https://www.microsoft.com/en-us/software-download/windows11.
- Scroll down to Download Windows 11 Disk Image (ISO) option and select Windows 11.
- Windows 11 Disk Image (ISO).
- Choose a language and click **Confirm**.
- It will take time for the file to download and while waiting for the completion of the download, let go to the **Registry** and make some changes.
- Type in **registry editor** on the **Search box** on the taskbar.
- Select the best match option, **Registry Editor.**
- And you need to move to a specific location in the **Registry Editor** interface.
- Then paste this HKEY_LOCAL_MACHINE\SYSTEM\Setup\MoSetup on the location field where you have the Computer.
- On the right-hand side of the screen where you have Name, Type, and Data, check if there is a value for **AllowUpgradesWithUnsupportedTPMOrCPU.** And if you did not see the value, right on the screen, tap **New** and select the option **DWORD (32-bit) Value.**
- Name the new value AllowUpgradesWithUnsupportedTPMOrCPU.
- Double-click on the new value, type 1 on the Value data field, and hit **OK**.
- Then close the **Registry Editor**.
- Double-click on the ISO file to open it after the download is finished.
- Select the file named **setup** with ISO file.

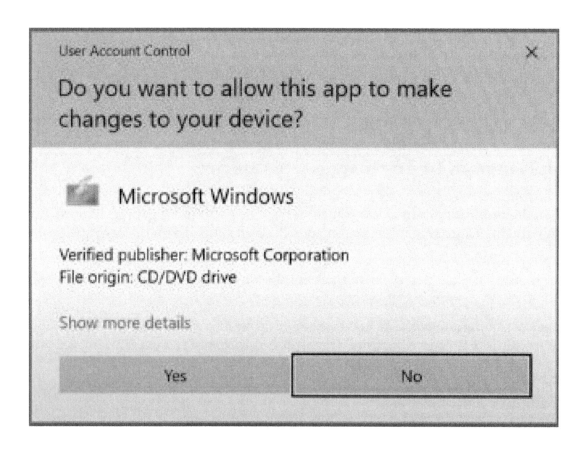

Click on **Yes** to initiate Windows 11 installation. It will take some time, but your PC will be running the Windows 11 operating system after the successful installation.

Chapter 2:
Configuring And Customizing Windows

Initial Look and Feel Compared To Windows 10

Unlike other older versions of Microsoft Windows Operating System, this new Windows, Windows 11 is just different. The Start menu of the Windows 11 Operating System is positioned at the center instead of the usual left-hand side of the Windows Operating System that has existed before now. The photo below indicates the position of the Start button in a PC running Windows 11 OS.

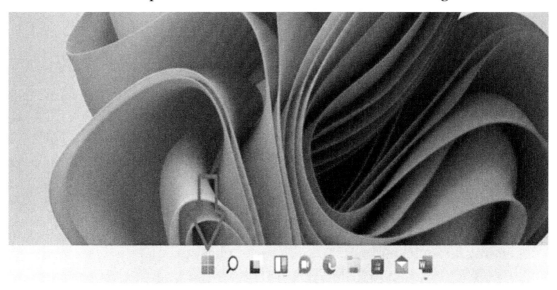

As a user of a Windows computer, most times, you select Start menu before you get to the other areas of your PC or apps. So, do not look for the Start button at the left, instead, get to it at the center just as you can see in the photo above. But know that irrespective of the position of the Start menu by default, you can change it to move to the left-hand side if you are more comfortable with that.

Using Windows - Programs And The Start Menu

How to Open and Manage Applications
If you want to open an application from the Start menu, click on the start menu and pick the application under All apps. If the application is also listed on the desktop and you want to launch it, you'd have to double-click instead of single-clicking, which will perform the same functions.

One of the features of the Windows 11 application is on the top right.

Now on a MacBook or in a macOS, those controls would be on the left-hand side. You can minimize the Apps by clicking on the little minus icon on the left, bringing the app down to the taskbar. You can preview or relaunch it by clicking on the app again. The other option is the maximize option. What you see as a partition on your screen is the new feature in Windows 11.

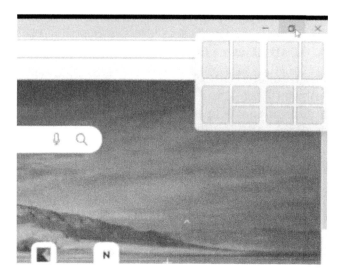

Now, this allows you with the emergence of larger desktops. Hold the mouse on the maximize icon and then select the partition to park the application in half of your screen or a certain position of your screen. So, if you want to adjust, click on maximize and move down to the corner of the screen. It gives you the option for a different display split part of the screen. Then you can have something else like files or Apps on a different part of the screen. So that's another option where you can adjust the display depending on what you want. To close the application, you can click on the x icon on the top right, which is standard with other versions of Windows.

How to Remove Unwanted Applications from Your Computer
When you buy even a new computer, there might be applications you don't want, and you want to speed up the computer and remove them. You get to see what applications are installed on the computer and can access them in a couple of ways. Go to the search option, just type Apps. Click on add and remove programs. It will list all the various programs that are installed on your computer.

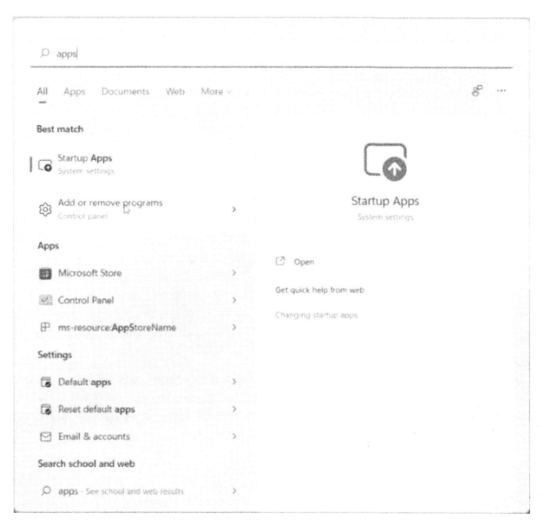

To remove any of those programs, go to any apps and click on the three dots. Then you can choose to modify it or uninstall it. When you modify it, it will select new parameters for the installation or reinstallation of the application.

How To Use The Start Screen Menu In Windows 11

One of the benefits of using Windows 11 is the Start menu. The menu is now a bit more intuitive with removing the Apps section. It's not much of a benefit, as the Start menu is now the same place it's always been, with adding some new features and a revamped search box. But there are still a few things that can be done with the start menu that you can't do with the app's view. If you want more information about the new Windows interface, continue reading.

One of the first things you'll probably notice about the Start menu in Windows 11 is that the background color has changed. While Windows 10 did have a different background color from the previous version, you could still change the color. In Windows 11, it's now black, which should make it easier to see what you're doing. While this is a minor change, having a single background color across the Start menu and other parts of Windows makes a lot of sense.

To change the background color, open the **Settings app**. Under **Personalization**, head to **Colors**. Click the **More Colors** option and then choose the color of your choice.

Customizing The Windows Start Menu And Taskbar

Restore The Classic Start Menu

One of the more noticeable changes in the Windows 11 Start menu is the removal of the Apps section. This is a change from Windows 10, where you could search for your apps as you were used to. While the classic Windows start menu had a search box, it was the search box of Windows 7. This means that you couldn't use it to search for your apps. Now that the Apps section is gone, you can't use it anymore. In its place, you get a tile for each app installed on your system. There is no more need to have a separate section for this.

Now, even though you can't search for your apps, the classic start menu lets you access the apps you use regularly. There are a few changes to the start menu on Windows 11. If you want to know how they work, head to the new Windows 11 Start menu section.

If you don't like the new look of the start menu, there are a few options that you can use. You can go to Settings and find the option to revert back to the old look. The classic start menu is still a part of Windows 11, just as it was in Windows 10. You just won't be able to get it from Settings anymore. In addition, if you don't like the look of the start menu in Windows 11, you can change the look of the Apps section. You just need to head to Settings and find the option to change your App icon.

How to Customize Start Screen

Windows 11 has some new features, such as Windows Holographic, and a new screen experience. Now that the modern desktop has replaced the Windows desktop, you will no longer see the Start Screen and the Metro screen. However, the new Modern UI still provides a Start Menu for you to customize, and you can customize the Start menu.

If you are new to Windows, you might not even know that you can customize the Start screen. This is a feature which is only available in Windows 10, and it can be found on the Start screen. If you are not already using Windows 10, you might not even have this feature.

However, in the latest Windows, there is an option to remove the Start menu, and the Start screen has become the only screen. You might not even know that the Start screen is customizable as well, but here is how you can customize the Start screen in Windows 11.

Step 1: *Go to start screen*

First, you need to go to the Start screen, which will be the only place where you will see the modern Start screen. You can find this by pressing the Windows key + S and then typing start.

Alternatively, you can open the Start screen by clicking the **Start button**.

Step 2: *Click on the Start button*

Once you open the Start screen, you will see two options next to the Microsoft logo. You can click on the Settings option, which will take you to a new settings screen. If you click on the Store option, you will see another screen where you can set your Store account.

The next screen is the modern search option. If you click on the new icon, this will launch the search interface on your Windows.

Step 3: Change your start screen appearance

Now that you have reached the modern start screen, you need to change the appearance.

You need to click on the **More tab** and then scroll down to the **Settings** option. You will then see options like **Time and Language, Privacy, Location**, and **Screen Savers**.

To change the Start screen **background**, you need to click on the new dropdown that says **Screen Saver**.

The next screen is the Screen Saver option, which will let you set your Start screen background, Windows theme, and screen saver. If you want a new background to be added, you must click on the **Screen Saver icon** and select the one you want.

If you do not like the icons on your Start screen, you can change that by clicking on the **App Icons link** and then select the apps you want.

You can click on the Small Apps link to change your Start screen tile. The next screen is called Tile Settings, and this will let you pick the apps you want to display as tiles.

To change your **Lock screen**, click on the **Lock screen link**. Here you can select the tiles and text colour, and set how long you want to be locked.

To change the **color** of your Start screen, click on the **Colors link**, and then scroll down to see a list of various colors you can choose from. To pick a color, you can click on the Color palette link and select the color you want.

To change your **desktop background**, click on the **Desktop link**.

Click on the Logon Screen Settings link to change your background for each of your Logon screens.

Pinning Applications to the Taskbar

The taskbar is a very useful feature of the Windows OS. Here, you can pin some important applications that you frequently use. For instance, if you always use Microsoft Office, you can pin shortcuts of Microsoft Word or Microsoft Excel to your taskbar. If you wish to have quick access to your favorite Internet browsers, you can also pin their shortcuts to the taskbar.

To pin any application you wish to your Windows 11 taskbar, you must first click the Start menu button. Doing this will display a window showing commonly used apps. In the search bar at the bottom of the window, type the name of the application you wish to pin to the taskbar.

You can also click **All Apps** to display all the applications that are installed on your computer. To pin an application, just right-click on it and select **Pin to taskbar**. By pinning an application to the taskbar, you can have quick access to that application anytime you wish to use it.

Pinning Applications to the Start Menu

You can also pin application shortcuts to the Start Menu. Users who want a clean taskbar prefer this option. By pinning an application to the **Start** menu, you will see them appear first when you click on Start.

Pinning an application to the Start menu is easy. First, click the Start menu button. Next, type the application name you wish to pin on the Search bar. For instance, if you wish to pin Zoom, just type "Zoom." This will bring up the Zoom application. Right-click on the application and click the option **Pin to Start**. This will immediately pin your application of choice to the Start menu.

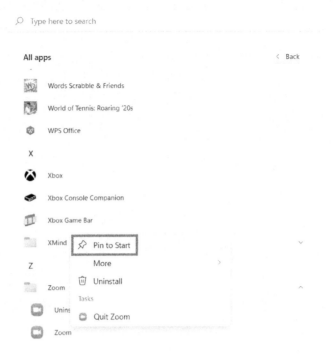

Every time you click the Start button, you will see the application you chose among the many applications in the Start menu. You can also unpin any application you no longer wish to see in the Start menu. To do that, just repeat the first two steps and then choose the option **Unpin from Start**. This will remove the application from the Start menu.

Changing The Date and Time

To set the date and time on your device, follow the simple steps mentioned below:

- Go to "Control Panel" option on the Search page.
- After opening the "Control panel" page, go to "Clock and Region" option.
- Go to "Set the time and date."
- Select "Change date and time" from the option.
- You will see the date and time in the system after tapping on OK.

Cortana — □ ×
...

Sign in to Cortana

Sign in

For the best experience, use your
work or school account

When you're signed in, Cortana learns how to better serve you by
using data such as your searches, calendar, contacts, and location.
Microsoft Privacy Statement

Cortana

Cortana by default on Windows 11 is disabled. You can activate Cortana on your Windows 11 by following the steps below:

- Go to the **Taskbar**, enter **Control panel** in the Search button, and click on **Open**

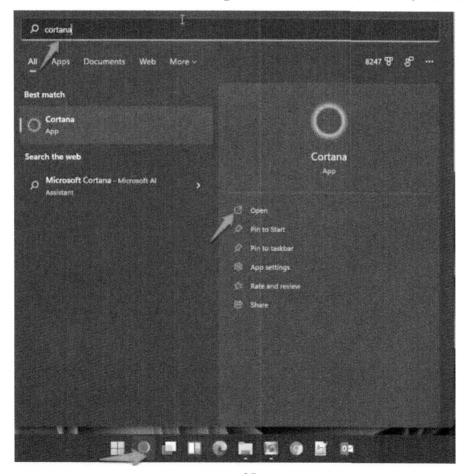

Click on the **Sign-in** button in the windows that pops up

Sign in with any of the options listed in the windows displayed and then click on **Continue.**

To set up the Cortana, click on the **three dots** at the left-hand side of the windows and click on **Settings**.

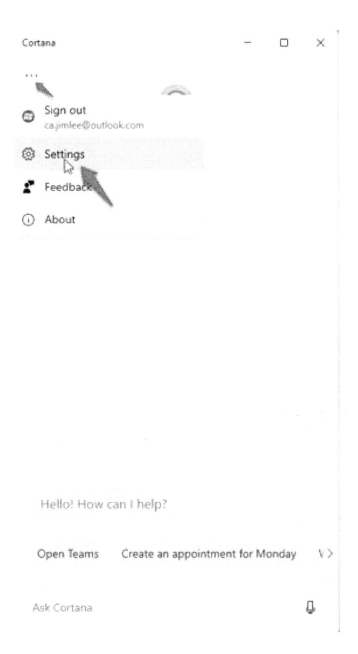

In this window, click on **Voice activation**

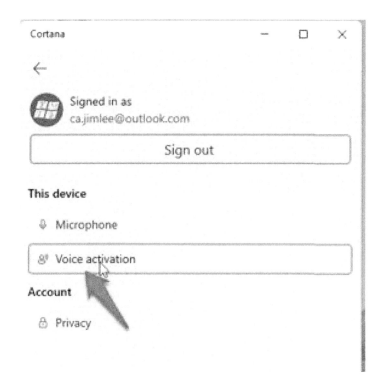

In the Voice activation windows that pops up, click on Voice activation privacy settings.

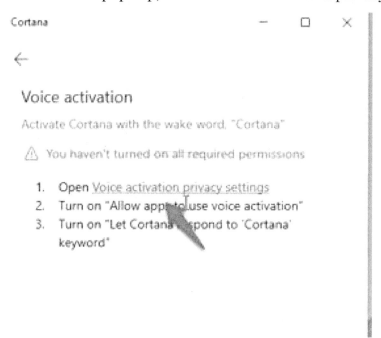

Another window is displayed where you turn on the **Cortana** toggle switch

After following these steps, go back to Cortana to start using it.

Windows Desktop

The Desktop is the starting point for everything you want to do on your computer. You can view the taskbar and Start menu from your desktop, as well as any other desktop shortcuts, your wallpaper, and open windows. The Desktop can show you important information about the status of your computer using the taskbar corner.

Changing Your Desktop Background

To change the desktop wallpaper in Windows 11, follow these steps:

1. Select the **Settings** option from the drop-down menu.
2. From the drop-down option, choose **Personalization**.
3. Click the Background page on the right side.
4. Under the **"Personalize your background"** option, choose the Picture option.
5. From the drop-down menu, choose **Browse Photos**.
6. For your desktop, choose a background image.
7. From the drop-down menu, choose a picture.
8. (Optional) In the Choose a fit for your desktop picture setting, choose **Fill** to ensure the image fits the whole screen. Other options are Fit, Stretch, Tile, Center, and Span.
9. You can also use the context menu to install a new desktop wallpaper by right-clicking a photo and choosing **Set as a desktop background**.

Changing Your Display Settings

The way your computer looks depends on the settings that control it. The display Settings of Windows 11 computers have to do with the elements of the computers. For instance, whether your computer screen appears bright or dull depends highly on the Display Settings. It is all about the brightness level you can control via the Display Settings.

To get to the Display Settings of your computer running Windows 11 Operating System, right-click on the desktop of your computer and select **Display Settings**, one of the options that will appear on the screen. The photo below is that of options made available on right clicking the desktop on my computer desktop.

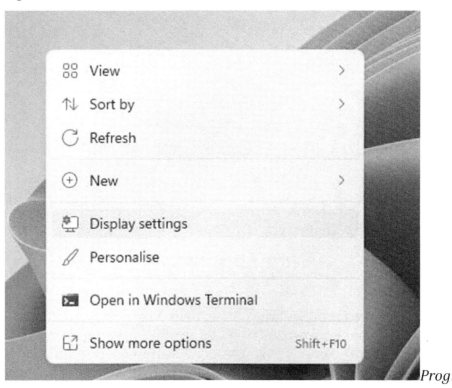

Progress

When you select **Display settings**, which is number 5 in the list of options above, a new page will open. The photo below is the new page that will open.

The

The above is part of the Display settings page. Some of the features there are what I taught you under Quick Action Center. But there is no problem guiding you on another approach to do the same thing. One of the beauties of Windows 11 is that there are many channels to get some tasks done.

Looking at the above image, if you want to increase or reduce the brightness of your computer screen, you can do that through the first tab named **Brightness**. Drag forward through the line to increase brightness, and backward to reduce brightness.

Also, the second tab is named **Night light**. With the night light feature, you can change the color of your computer screen so that it will be warm to the eyes when using your computer at night. Toggle on the button to turn it on. This feature allows users to fall asleep easily after using their computers for a long time at night.

The third tab in the Display settings is named **HDR**. The HDR has imparted in games and videos that are displayed on your computer screen. It imparts video game images in a great way. When you click that tab, you can change the images displayed in games and videos you watch on your computer.

Tab 4 under the Display settings and category Scale & layout is named **Scale**. When you click the **Scale** tab, you will have access to the tools you need to change the size of text, apps and other functions available on your computer. By default, the scale is set at 100%. That scale of 100% is recommended for most computers, but some expert users of Microsoft Windows sometimes change it based on what they are doing on their computers at a particular time.

Display resolution is another tab under **Display settings**. A resolution has to do with the pixels that appear in images. Just know that this has an impact on the image qualities displayed on your computer screen. I recommend you place the display resolution of your Windows 11 to the one chosen for you by Microsoft on the installation of your new Operating System.

Display Orientation is another tab under the Display settings of Windows 11. When you click the dropdown at the right-hand end of that tab, you are given between Landscape and Portrait to choose from. Whichever one you choose will affect how things are displayed on your computer screen.

The tab number 7 is named **Multiple displays**. The multiple displays is important if you use more than one computer monitor. If your computer running Windows 11 Operating System is running two monitors, you can add the second monitor through multiple displays and then start using it. Also, when you click the dropdown at the **Multiple displays**, you will see some options: **Remember Window locations based on monitor connection** and **Minimize Windows when a monitor is disconnected**. These two options are checked at default, but you can decide to uncheck the two or any. But know that this is important f you have two monitors connected to your PC, but if not, do not bother yourself. Just like me, my computer uses only one monitor, which is the main one that comes with my computer. In that situation, I do not have anything to worry about on the **Multiple displays** tab.

Changing Themes, Colors, And Sounds

Themes or Colors

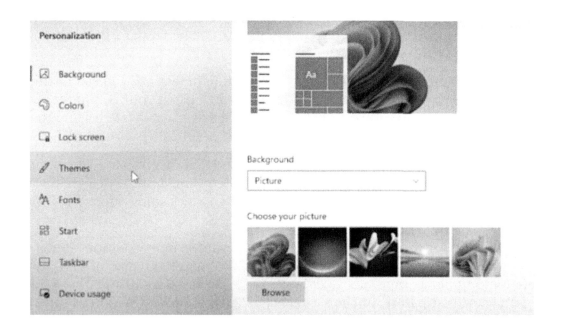

Themes are now called Colors in Windows 11. It is no longer possible to do any of that in Windows 11 though.

The new feature is called **Colors,** which allows you to use various colors to match your personal design needs. By simply clicking on the color you want, you can download the colors that Microsoft used for the default colors in Windows 11.

You can see the colors available by clicking on the **cog** on the top right-hand side of the **Start Screen.**

There are no more themes in Windows 11; the whole concept of themes is just one big color picker.

If you want one of the new colors, you need to click on the cog icon on the top right, go into Personalization, and click on the option called **Color Settings**.

You will see a list of the new colors, with a button beside it for each color. Simply click on the button and you will see a screen where you can choose your colors.

(You can also add the Colors from the top right cog option by going to **Personalization,** then clicking on the **Colors Settings** Icon, then clicking the **More** button on the right side, then selecting the option for **More Colors** and then clicking the button beside each color you want.)

Step 1: Open the **Settings** application.

Step 2: Click **Personalization** and select the **Details view.**

Step 3: Click the **gear icon** () next to the Color group and then select **Color.**

Step 4: Under the **Themes tab**, click **Colors and** select the theme you want to use.

Sounds

Windows 11's system noises have been synchronized to match its visual attractiveness and a softer and more fluid design. As a result, the alerts on the new Windows sound more soothing.

How to Change the Sounds on a Windows 11 Computer

Windows 11 is the first version of Windows to provide separate sound effects for **light** and **dark** settings. The noises for both modes are not wholly different, even if they are distinct.

The **light mode** features brighter and louder sounds than the **dark mode**, however, both sound profiles have been engineered to be calmer and gentler by Microsoft.

However, if you wish to edit or add additional sounds to the mix, follow these steps:

Go to the taskbar's Search icon and type in **"sound settings."**

Under Best match, select **Sound settings**, or click **Open** on the right pane under Sound settings. By right-clicking on the Sound icon on the taskbar and choosing **Sound settings**, you can also go to the **System sound settings** page.

Scroll down to the **Advanced section** and choose **More sound options** from the drop-down menu.

The Sounds window will appear with numerous settings. The Program Events list will appear under Program Events when you choose the Sounds option at the top of the window. Calendar Reminder, Low Battery Alarm, New Mail Notification, and other events will be included.

Now choose the program event which you want to adjust the sound.

Next, choose the menu arrow next to the name of the default Windows Background sound. It will bring up a menu of sound selections for you to choose from.

How to Set Your Preferred Sound as a Notification Alert

If you don't like the sound choices Windows provides, you may alter them to something else. Ensure the sound you wish to add is in WAV format before you begin since Windows will only accept WAV files as system sounds.

To store a customized sound, open the File Explorer by clicking Browse in the sound settings. After that, choose the custom **WAV sound effect** you want to utilize. To save the sound, click **Apply and OK** after clicking **Access** to open the sound settings.

How to Disable the Startup Sound in Windows 11

Microsoft has removed the ability to customize the Windows 11 Startup Sound. You may, however, disable the default starting sound if you don't want to hear it every time you power on your computer.

- Look for **Sound Options > More sound settings > Sounds** will take you to the above-mentioned sound options page.
- Simply uncheck the blue box next to **Play Windows Startup sound** in the Program Events window. The Startup sound will also be disabled.

How to Turn Off Windows 11 System Sounds

There may be instances when you need to concentrate on a job and don't want any interruptions. This covers turning off the system noises in Windows 11.

- You can quickly **turn off system noises** if you desire some silence. To go to the sound settings page, search for **Sound settings** > **More sound options** > **Sounds**.
- Select **No Sounds** from the Sound Scheme drop-down menu. You will no longer be troubled by any system noises while your work after this is completed.

Screen Savers

To change settings of the screen saver, Go to Settings > Personalization > Lock screen, and choose Screen saver settings. In the Screen Saver Settings window, pick a screen saver from the drop-down list.

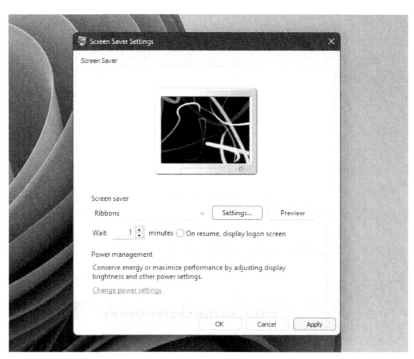

Windows Power Settings

There is more to the Power button of your personal computer than most people think. You can turn your computer on and off with it, and you can also use it to log out of your computer. The Power button can be accessed via the **Start** menu. You will find the power button on your Windows 11 OS at the bottom right corner of the Start menu page. As you can see, this is different from previous versions, where the power button is found at the bottom left corner of the screen, right at the exact location where you'll find the Start button.

There are a few things you can do through the power button. When you click the power icon, the options for **Sleep**, **Shut down**, and **Restart** will appear.

The **Sleep** option is for when you're working and wish to take a break but don't want to shut down your computer completely. When you put your computer to sleep, the computer won't shut down, but the apps and programs become inactive. When you're ready to work again, you can come back and just click the mouse for the computer to "wake up." You will have to click the power button on your CPU on a desktop computer. The main difference is that your computer won't go through the entire process of booting up again.

To put your computer in sleep mode, just click the **Start** button, click the **Power** button, and then select **Sleep**.

Another option you will find when you click the power button is **Shut down**. This will completely turn off your computer. Unlike when you put your computer in sleep mode when you want to use your computer again, you will have to push the power button on your CPU, and your computer will go through the entire booting process. This usually takes just a little bit longer than when you simply wake your computer up from sleep mode.

Restart is another option you can access through the **Power button**. Sometimes you will notice your computer slowing down a bit, and apps and programs don't respond as quickly as they should. This is where the restart button comes in. Restarting your computer will cause it to reboot, and if there are updates that may need to be installed, the computer will install them during this process.

Hibernate Mode

If you've been a Windows OS user for a long time now, you're probably familiar with the hibernate function. You may wonder why it's not available in recent versions of Windows operating systems. By default, **Hibernate** is disabled on Windows 11. This is why you don't see this option on the Power button.

If you wish to enable **Hibernate**, go to **Start** and type "Control Panel" in the search bar. The Control Panel icon will appear as you type. Click on the icon, and a new page will appear.

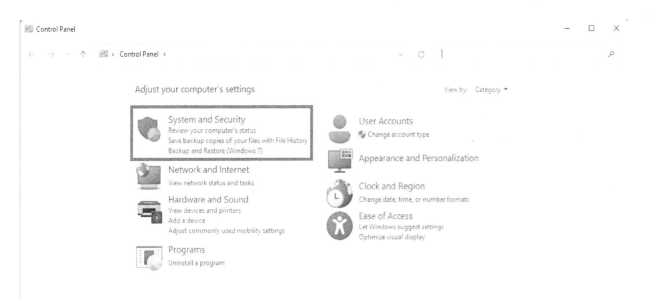

Click System and Security, and under Power Options, click Change what the power buttons do.

This will open another page where you will need to check a box to enable Hibernate as shown below.

Define power buttons and turn on password protection

Choose the power settings that you want for your computer. The changes that you make to the settings on this page apply to all of your power plans.

🛡 Change settings that are currently unavailable

Power and sleep buttons and lid settings

		🔋 On battery		🔌 Plugged in	
⏻	When I press the power button:	Sleep	∨	Sleep	∨
◉	When I press the sleep button:	Sleep	∨	Sleep	∨
📴	When I close the lid:	Sleep	∨	Sleep	∨

Shut-down settings

☑ Turn on fast start-up (recommended)
    This helps start your PC faster after shut-down. Restart isn't affected. Learn More
☑ Sleep
    Show in Power menu.
☐ Hibernate
    Show in Power menu.
☑ Lock
    Show in account picture menu.

Save changes   Cancel

In the screenshot, you will notice that Hibernate is not checked under Shut-down settings. To enable Hibernate, check the box beside it and click Save Changes at the bottom of the page.

Now, Hibernate is enabled on your computer. Understand that this option is similar to Sleep, so when you hibernate your computer, although it uses less power than sleep. Use this option if you wish to take a break from using your computer but don't want to wait for your computer to reboot when you get back. Since it uses less power than putting your PC to sleep, use it whenever you want to conserve battery power.

Windows Control Panel

A control panel is a digital dashboard, a central location where all settings can be quickly found and accessed. Control panels can be used on the computer desktop or in the web browser as well. The term has been used to describe online shopping systems as early as the mid-1990s.

The Windows 11 control panel is accessible via the Windows key **Win + S,** where you can search the **Control Panel** tile and open it. It is one of the most visited places on your Windows PC, as you can control all the basic settings of the system using the control panel. The Control Panel has been revamped to make your Windows experience faster and easier without you needing to utilize it for some operations. With Windows 10, you were left with a pretty sparse control panel: you can tweak the operating system to a degree, but there are only a handful of settings available that might make sense to you or your device. Windows 11 is a much better OS to look for settings, with more options available under each heading.

How To Customize The Lock Screen

You may also change the backdrop and alerts on the Lock screen. Follow these instructions to modify the Windows 11 Lock screen:

- Navigate to Settings.
- Select Personalization.
- On the right, select the Lock screen page.

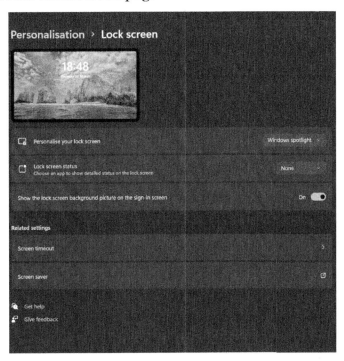

Several parameters may be customized as part of the Lock screen settings, including the background picture and app status. The Windows spotlight is the default option under the Lock screen, and it lets you display a new backdrop each time you sign in to your account. You may, however, utilize the Picture option to display a custom picture or the Slideshow option to rotate a collection of photographs.

47

When you choose Slideshow, the system will load the photographs from the Pictures folder. However, you may add and remove the directories you want to display. You may even integrate your computer's and OneDrive's camera roll folders.

In addition, when the device is dormant, there is an option to display the Lock screen with a slideshow. Some programs can display extensive status information, which you can customize by choosing the app from the Lock screen status drop-down box.

Chapter 3:
User Account

User Account Types

Windows 11 has two types of accounts; Administrator Accounts and Standard Account Accounts. Standard Account Users are limited in terms of what they can do as compared to Administrator accounts. For example, Standard account users can only perform tasks they are assigned. They can't change any system settings, such as Windows Firewall settings or other power management features, or modify preferences in Windows Store apps.

If you need a Standard Account, access a particular set of executable files, go to Settings > Control Panel > Ease of Access Center and click 'Change how users access this computer.'

You will see a list of apps that require administrator privileges.

Select the app and click the 'Change' button.

The application will be marked as administrator-only and will not open unless you're logged in with an administrator account. You can also set your local user account permissions as per your requirements by going to Settings > Accounts > Your account > Manage Permissions for your user account.

You can use administrator accounts to manage your device's applications, users, and various system settings. They have full access to your device's files, programs, and resources. If you want one user account to have administrator privileges, you must switch from Standard User to Administrator User.

You can create multiple user accounts on your device anytime by clicking on the Settings application. Then select Users and then Add New User. Add a user account by giving it a name and choosing an image or picture for it.

To create a Windows 11 user account, you must have at least one administrator account.

After creating an administrator account, you can create additional user accounts by using another account on your machine and changing the user's type to Standard User. Then users can give it a particular name and choose an image or picture for it. You can use the Task Manager if you want to switch between users on your device.

To do this, click the Start button and then click Task Manager. On the left-hand side of the Task Manager are all of your user accounts and their respective processes. You can switch to any of those accounts by clicking on it.

Creating User Accounts

Ensure you are logged in as an administrator, go to "**Family and other people**" in your account settings, and click on "**Add someone else to this PC**".

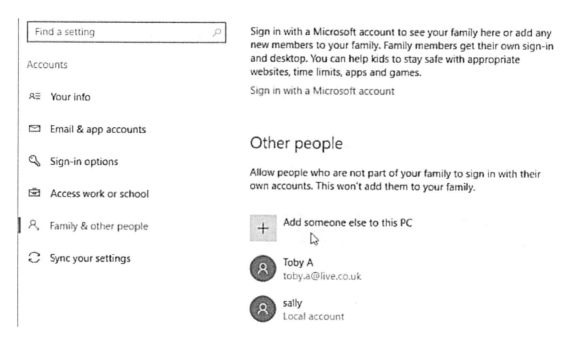

You have some options when you do this. One of the options is to specify the person's email address or phone number. That email address may be a Microsoft account email address or it could be some other email address. If you do not have the person's details, you can click on the button that says, "**I don't have this person's sign-in information**".

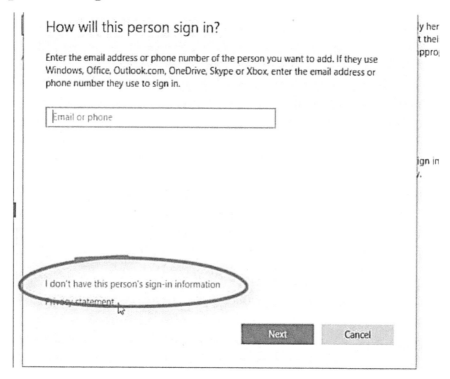

In this case, you would have to set the user off with a local account. When you click on that it will take you to another window that will help you get started with creating an account for the user. In this case, click on the button that says, "**Add a user without a Microsoft account**".

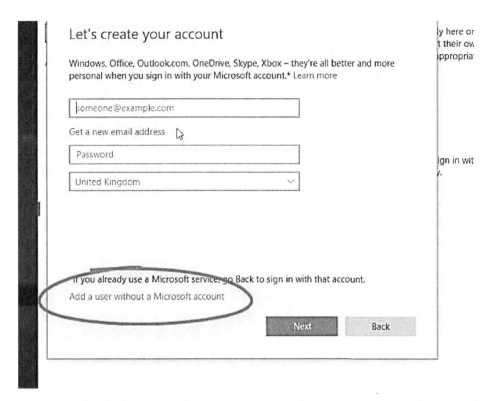

In this situation, all you will do is put in the username and enter a password. Once the account is set up, you can tell the user his login details to enable him to log in and set up whatever other information he wants to set up. Click on "**Next**", and the new user account is now set up with a local account.

If you want to see someone's Microsoft account and you know the person's email address or phone number, then you could fill in the appropriate boxes in the sequence.

Changing Passwords

In this section, you will learn how to change your Windows password. There are a couple of ways to change it. If you're working in a corporate environment or connected to a network, you will change the password through the IT department's tools. However, in most cases, like a network account, you can change your Windows password by pressing Ctrl Alt Delete on your computer, and then a prompt like an image below will appear.

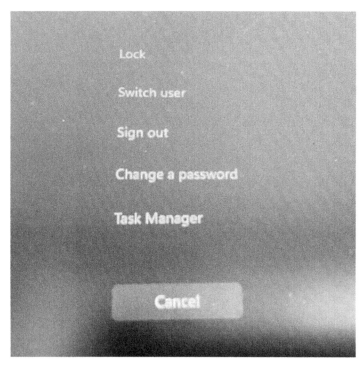

Then you can click on change password, put in your old password followed by the new password and confirm the new password. That is the quickest and easiest way to change the password.

The other options are also on the Search. If you go to Search, you have more clicks involved in the procedure on the change password, but you'd still reach the same conclusion.

Switching Users

A friend of yours may visit one day and feel like using your computer. He may need to switch users before he starts what he wants to do. How will you now log out for the new user to login?

If you want to sign out from your computer running Windows 11 Operating System, take these steps:

- Click the **Start** menu of your computer
- Click the **Account name** of your computer and you will see some options just as you can see in the photo below.

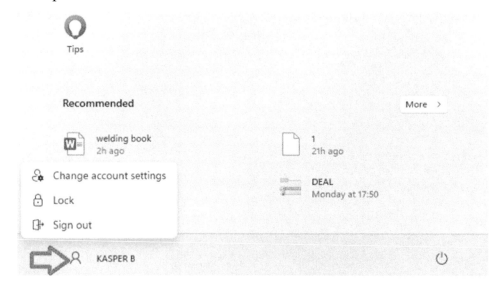

- Click the **Sign out** option. On taking this last step, you will be logged out of your computer and another user can then sign into the computer to carry out any task he or she wants to do.

Creating A Password Reset Disk

This section will go through how to change the windows 11 default password policy.

- Click on the Windows logo
- Click on All Apps
- Scroll down and find out Windows tools
- Click on Windows tools
- Double-click on local security policy

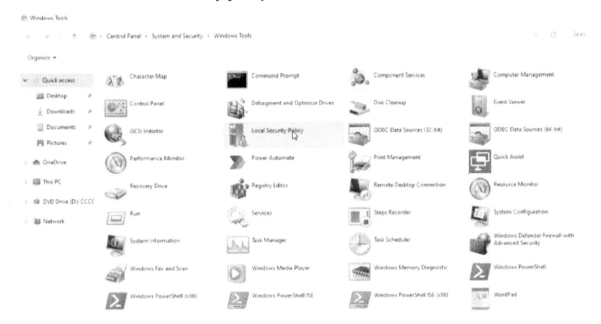

- Select and expand Account policy

- Select Password policy

You have all password options which the Administrator can change.

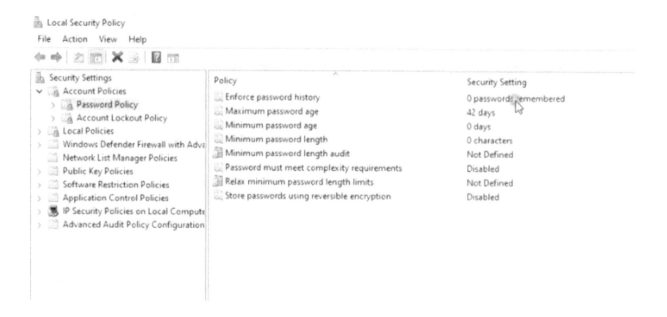

The first option is to enforce password history. That means the enforced password history policy setting limits the number of unique new passwords that must be linked with a user account before an old password can be reused.

If you do not set the minimum password age, users can change their password several times in a row as needed to reuse their original password. Leave the option as default.

The second option is maximum password age. That means the maximum password age policy setting determines the time in days the password can be used before the System asks the User to change it. For example, you can set passwords to expire after several days between 1 and 999, or you can state that passwords never expire by setting the number of days to zero. By default is 42 days. Leave as default.

The third option is minimum password age. This means the minimum password age policy setting determines when a password must be used before the User can change it. For example, you can set a value between 1 and 998 days or allow password changes instantly by setting the number of days to zero.

- Double clicks on it. You can set 30 days of the minimum password age
- Click on Apply
- Click on Ok

The fourth option is minimum password length. This means setting the minimum password length to at least a value of 8. if the number of characters is zero, no password is required. An eight-character password is recommended in most environments because it's long enough to provide adequate security and still short enough for users to remember easily.

- Double click on it and set 3 characters for minimum password length.
- Click on Apply
- Click on Ok

The fifth option is password must meet complexity requirements. It means a password made up of alphabets, symbols and numerics is called a complexity password. By default, it is disabled in the password policy. However, if you want to enable it, you can double-click on it.

- Close Local security policy
- Close Windows tools
- Right-click on the Windows logo and select Run
- Type gpupdate, then press Enter

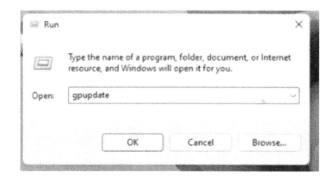

- Right-click on This PC and select Manage
- expand Local Users and Groups
- Select Users
- Right-click on Users and select New User
- Fill User information
- Fill Password
- Fill Confirm password
- Click on Create

It will show an error message that the password does not meet the password policy requirement.

Set to character password at the time of user creation for checking purpose that's why it's showing error.

- Click on Ok

Now this time, set a 3-character password

- Fill Confirm password

- Click on Create

- Click on Close

The User is created with no error showing because you choose minimum of 3 characters in the password policy.

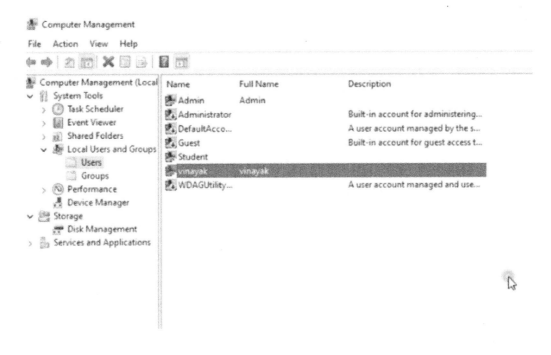

Now you have learned how to change the default password policy of windows 11.

Chapter 4:
Installing Devices

Installing Printers/Scanners

Windows 11 is good at automatically identifying any network or wireless printers and will make sure to download all of the drivers needed to run the equipment properly. To add a new printer or scanner, begin by making sure it is powered up and plugged into the computer or network or the wireless connection is turned on correctly. Then visit Settings > Bluetooth & devices > Printers & scanners. Click the Refresh button so that Windows 11 can begin searching for the device. You should see the name of your printer or scanner appear in the list. Click on your printer or scanner, and it will be installed and ready to use.

If you do not see your printer or scanner appear in the list, you will have to try another option. This may happen with older models. Click "" The printer I want isn't listed" to add one manually. Follow the prompts on the screen to connect the printer or scanner and install all the necessary drivers. If you have a wireless printer, you must ensure it is connected to the same network as your computer.

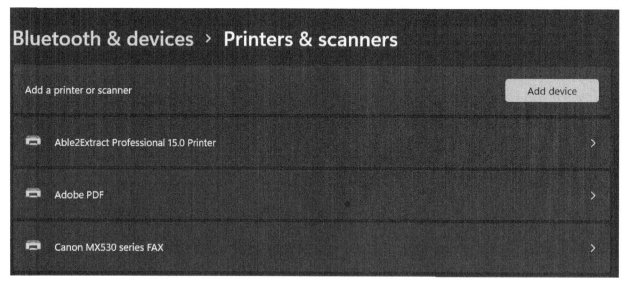

Connecting A Smartphone to Your Computer

The Windows 11 Phone App helps carry out some important functions of your phone such as sending messages, making and receiving calls, receiving notifications, and accessing your photos, without removing your phone from your pocket or bag. With this app feature, you can access your smartphone's messages, photos, and notifications and make phone calls.

If you do already have this feature on your computer, you can get the **"Your Phone"** app from Microsoft App Store.

When you open the app, Windows will want to know your phone type. Click on the Android or iPhone button as it applies to you and click the **"Continue"** button to proceed.

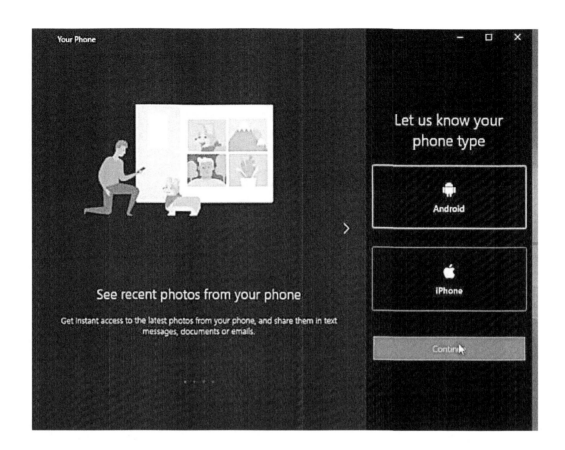

Now, you will be required to sign in with your Microsoft account. Enter your sign-in details to continue.

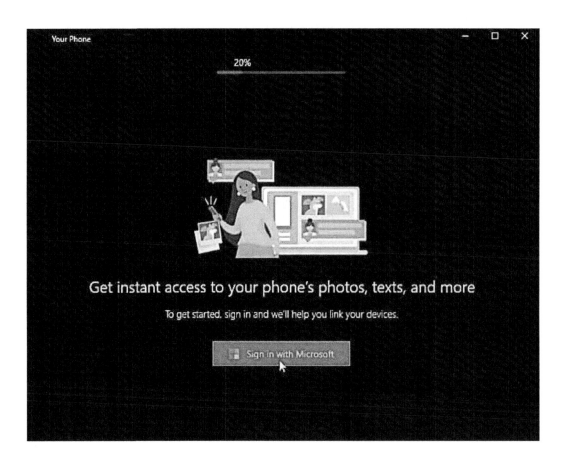

You may get a window telling you to **"Use this account everywhere on your device"**. Click **"Next"** to continue.

This may take some minutes to set up, after which your Phone app comes up. Now, you will need to link your smartphone.

In your Google play store, search for **"Your Phone Companion"** and install.

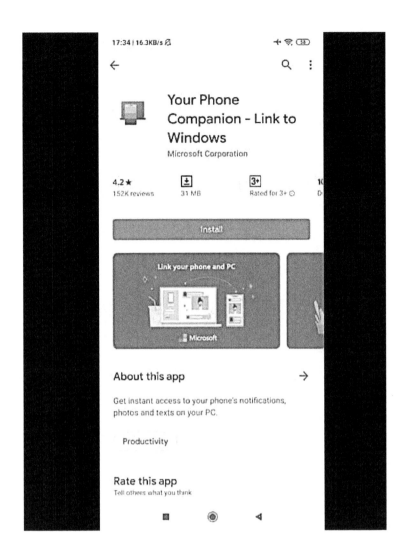

After installation, sign in with your Microsoft account.

Allow the app to access your phone's photos, media, files and other permission and press "**continue**".

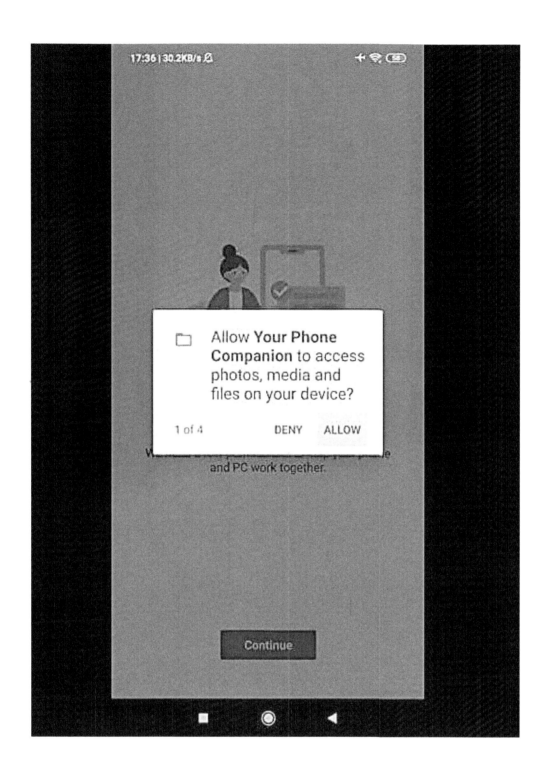

Now, go to your computer and you will see that your computer is trying to connect with your phone. This will require one more permission on your smartphone, so go to your smartphone and click on "**Allow**".

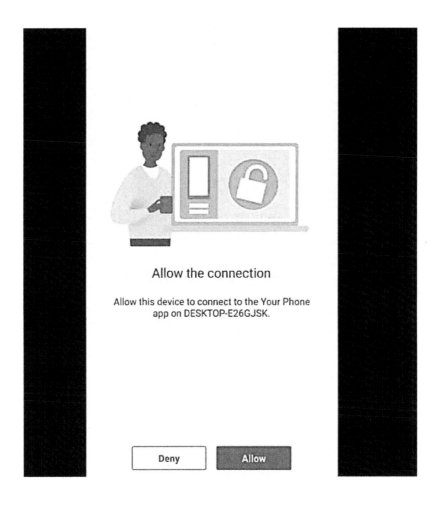

Allow the connection

Allow this device to connect to the Your Phone
app on DESKTOP-E26GJSK.

Deny   Allow

You will get a notification that your phone and PC are linked.

Your phone and PC are linked

If you uninstall this app, you might need to link
your phone and PC again.

You have successfully connected to your computer. From your PC, you can now access your smartphone.

Mouse Settings

Setting The Mouse for Left-handed People

By default, the mouse's primary button is set to the left button because most users use the right hand. Probably you are a left-handed person; you can change the mouse primary button from left to right. To do this follow the steps below:

- Go to the **Start Menu** and click on the **Setting** icon
- In the **Settings** menu, go to **Bluetooth & devices** and click on **Mouse** on the right-hand side.

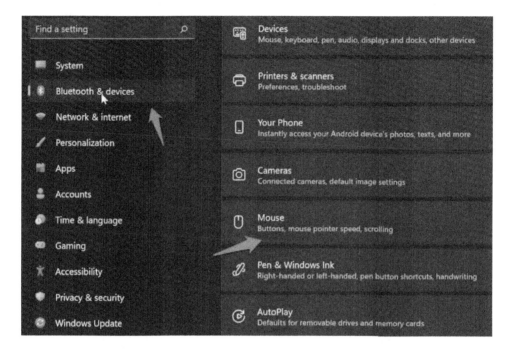

- In **the Primary mouse** button, choose the **Right** option

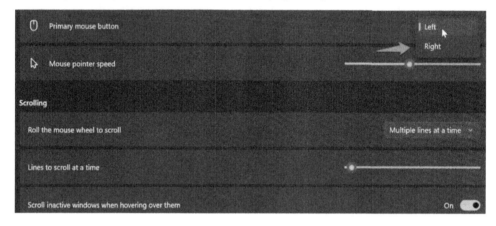

Changing the Color of the Mouse Cursor on Windows 11
To change the color of the mouse cursor of your PC, follow the steps provided below:

- Go to the **Start** button and click on the **Setting** icon
- In the **Settings** menu, go to **Accessibility**, click on **Mouse pointer and touch** at the right-hand side.

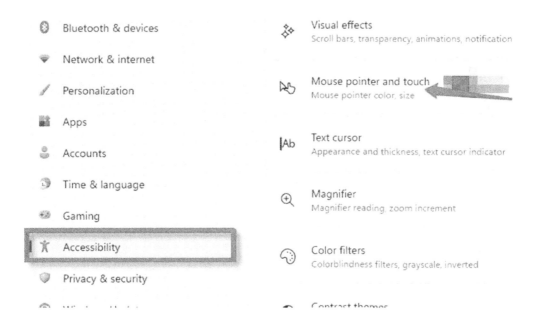

- In the **Mouse pointer and touch** option, select the color you want. You can also choose a color from the plus sign beside the **Choose another color** option.

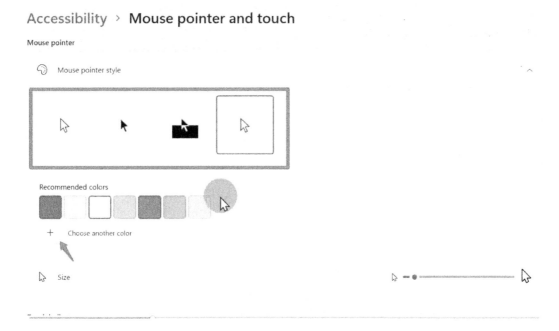

Changing the Mouse Pointer Size

To adjust the size of the mouse pointer, follow the steps provided below:

- Go to the **Start** button and click on the **Setting** icon

- In the **Settings** menu, go to **Accessibility**, click on **Mouse pointer and touch** at the right-hand side.

- In the **Mouse pointer and touch** option, move the slider in the Size to make changes to the mouse pointer. To increase the size of the pointer, move the slider to the right and to decrease the size of the pointer, move the slider to the left.

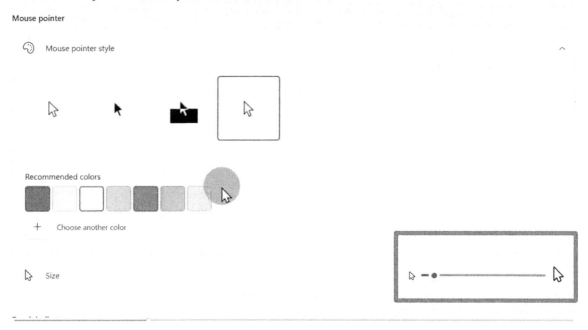

Changing the Mouse Cursor Scheme

The default scheme of a mouse cursor is a white arrow symbol. However, the mouse scheme can be changed. To do this, follow the steps below:

- Go to the **Start** button and click on the **Setting** icon
- In the **Settings** menu, go to **Accessibility,** click on **Mouse pointer and touch** at the right-hand side.
- In the **Mouse pointer and touch** option, click on Mouse under **Related settings**

Accessibility > Mouse pointer and touch

+ Choose another color

Size

Touch indicator

Touch indicator
Show a circle on the screen where I touch it

☐ Make the circle darker and larger

Related settings

Mouse
Mouse pointer speed, primary button, scrolling

Text cursor
Text cursor indicator, thickness

Touchpad
Gestures, sensitivity

- Click on Additional mouse settings under Related settings

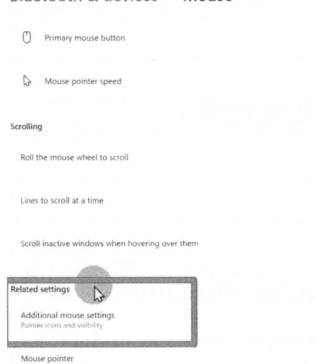

Bluetooth & devices > Mouse

Primary mouse button

Mouse pointer speed

Scrolling

Roll the mouse wheel to scroll

Lines to scroll at a time

Scroll inactive windows when hovering over them

Related settings

Additional mouse settings
Pointer icons and visibility

Mouse pointer
Pointer size and color

•

- In the **Mouse Properties** dialog box, go to the **Pointer tab,** and select an option in the **Scheme drop-down** menu

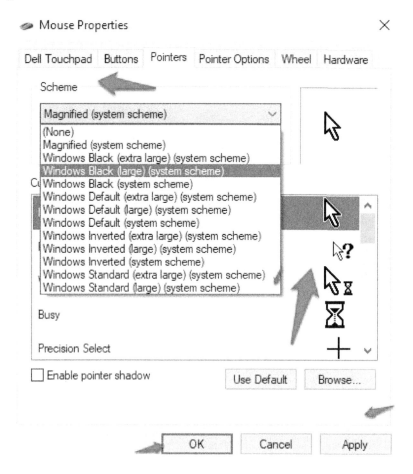

- Click on the **Ok** and **Apply** buttons when you are done to effect the change.

Changing the Mouse Pointer Motion Speed on Windows 11
You can also change the movement of the mouse in response to the speed of the cursor. To do this, follow the steps given below

- Go to the **Start** button and click on the **Setting** icon
- In the **Settings** menu, go to **Accessibility**, click on **Mouse pointer and touch** at the right-hand side.
- In the **Mouse pointer and touch** option, click on Mouse under **Related settings**
- Click on **Additional mouse** settings under **Related settings**
- In the **Mouse Properties** dialog box, click on the **Pointer Options** tab
- In the **Motion** section, move the pointer speed to the right to increase the speed and to the left to decrease the speed.
- After these are done, click on the **Apply** and **Ok** button.

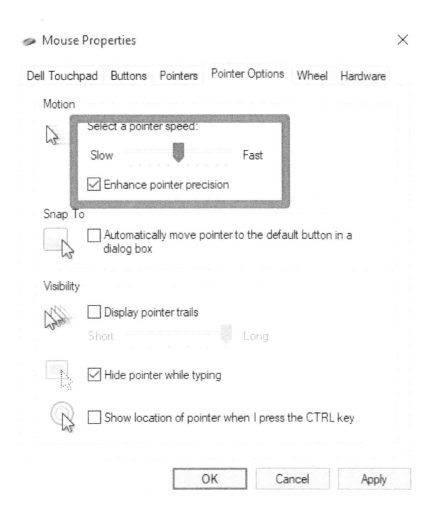

Making the Mouse Pointer More Evident on Windows 11

Sometimes the mouse looks as if it was not on the screen. In this situation, making the mouse pointer more visible is the way out. You can make the mouse pointer more visible by

- Highlighting the Mouse Cursor

- Showing Pointer Trails

Highlighting the Mouse Cursor

Highlighting the mouse pointer lets you know where the mouse will be next by using the Ctrl key. To highlight the mouse cursor, follow the steps below

- Go to the **Start** button and click on the **Setting** icon
- In the **Settings** menu, go to **Accessibility**, click on **Mouse pointer and touch** at the right-hand side.
- In the **Mouse pointer and touch** option, click on Mouse under **Related settings**
- Click on **Additional mouse** settings under **Related settings**
- In the **Mouse Properties** dialog box, click on the **Pointer Options** tab
- In the Visibility section, mark the checkbox **Show location of pointer when I press the CTRL key**
- After these are done, click on the **Apply** and **Ok** button.

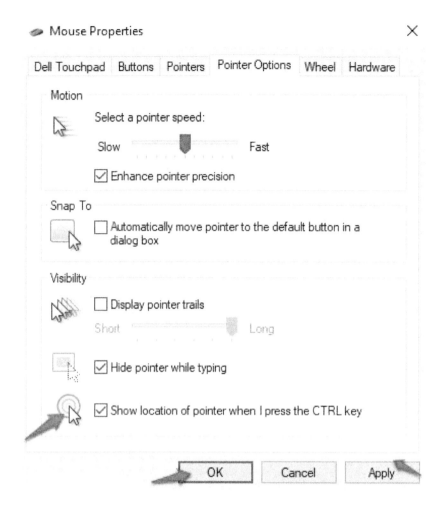

Showing Pointer Trails

Another way to make the pointer more visible is to enable the pointer trails. The pointer trails appear like fading mouse cursors accompanying the real cursor. To enable the pointer trails, follow the steps below:

- Go to the **Start** button and click on the **Setting** icon
- In the **Settings** menu, go to **Accessibility**, click on **Mouse pointer and touch** at the right-hand side.
- In the **Mouse pointer and touch** option, click on Mouse under **Related settings**
- Click on **Additional mouse** settings under **Related settings**
- In the **Mouse Properties** dialog box, click on the **Pointer Options** tab
- In the **Visibility** section, mark the checkbox Display **pointer trails**
- After these are done, click on the **Apply** and **Ok** button

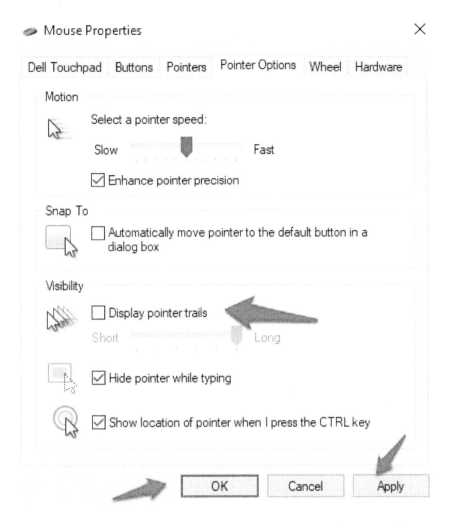

Enabling the Mouse Keys on Windows 11

Rather than using the mouse to move the cursor on your PC, you can use the mouse keys to move the cursor. To do this, follow the steps provided below:

- Go to the **Start** button and click on the **Setting** icon
- In the **Settings** menu, go to **Accessibility** and click on **Mouse** on the right-hand side.

- In the **Mouse** options, turn on the **Mouse keys** toggle switch. When the Mouse key is enabled, the following settings can be used.
- Only use Mouse Keys when Num Lock is on
- Show the Mouse Keys icon on the taskbar
- Hold the Ctrl key to speed up and the Shift key to slow down the cursor speed.
- Change how fast the printer moves when using mouse keys
- Change how quickly the printer starts & stops when using the mouse key

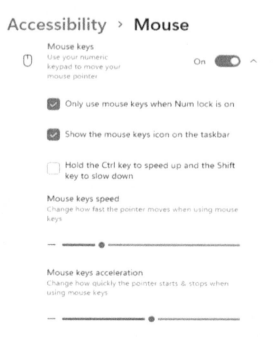

Installing USB Devices

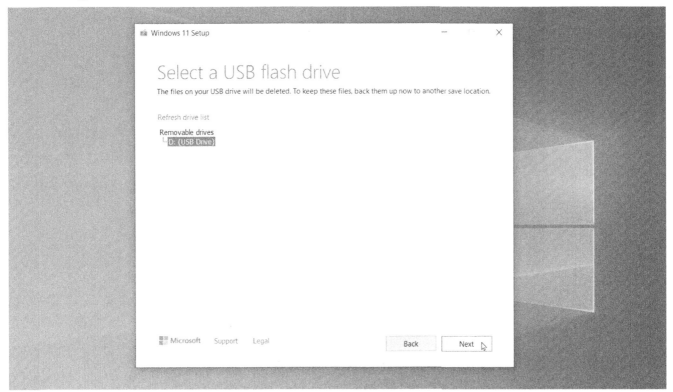

If you want to make it easy to connect devices to your PC, you can add them in the same way you already do: in the Start Menu.

To connect devices, right-click on the Start button, then click Devices and choose to Add a new device.

All devices can now be found in the Start Menu in a new tab, so you can add and connect them without opening the Programs or Features section.

The Add button will appear at the bottom of the page. If you want to change the name or type of a device, type it in and hit Add again to format it.

If you have a particular setting for a device you want to keep, right-click it and select Properties, then click the Additional Devices tab at the top right of the page and add it.

You can also use the button to automatically connect a device or choose to connect it manually. For example, if you want to connect your laptop to a printer automatically, you can do this from the Printing options in the Devices and Features pane.

If you want to give a PC a wireless network connection, choose Devices, select the Wireless and Networking tab, and click Wireless Network. Then specify the network connection type: wireless, wired, or Ethernet.

Dual Monitor Setup

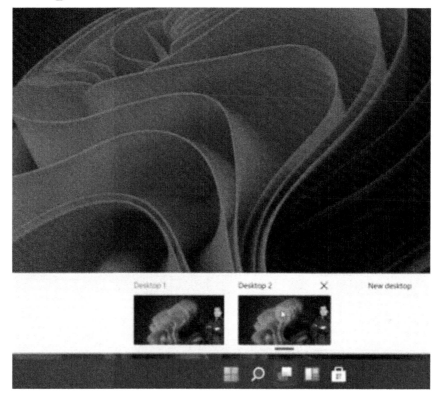

Have you ever wanted to use your dual monitors on Windows 11, to have 2 monitors to display 2 different apps/windows side-by-side? It is like having dual desktops, but what does it look like to set up? This topic will help you set up dual.

To enable this dual monitor setup:

- You'll have to navigate the Settings app and click **"Displays."**
- Once you've opened the **Display page,** you'll see the part that says **"Make this my main display",** and you'll notice the other monitor is now active.
- Now, when you're finished configuring, click on the **"Apply"** button, and you'll be able to apply the settings.

Chapter 5:
How To Install Any Software

How To Install Google Chrome

Chrome is not included in Windows 11. You have to download it if you want to install and use it. Once downloaded, you may also set it to your Windows 11 default web browser.

On the taskbar, click Microsoft Edge to download Google Chrome.

Then click the following link to download Chrome:

google.com/chrome

Click the **Download button** on the Download page.

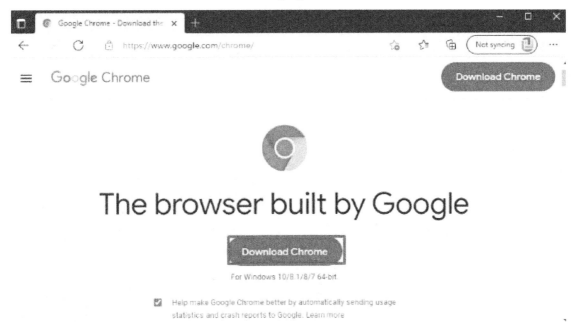

Next, when requested, click the **Accept and Install option**.

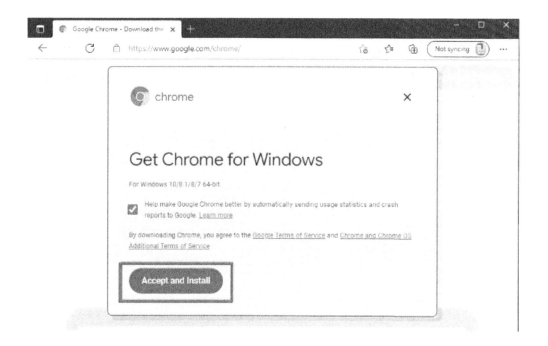

Once the file has been downloaded, go to the Downloads folder in File Explorer and double-click the installer to start Chrome's installation.

The Chrome installer should begin installing Google Chrome in a few seconds. After the installation is complete, Google Chrome should launch and be ready for use.

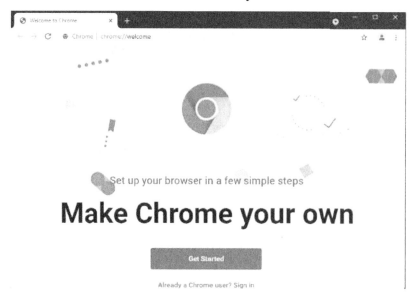

How To Make Google Chrome Your Default Browser

When Windows 11 was originally released to the public, it was impossible to establish Google Chrome as the default browser with one or two clicks, as was possible in previous versions of Windows. Previously, users could choose Google Chrome as their default browser, and any file extension linked with web browsers would immediately open in Google Chrome.

1. On your Windows 11 device, go to the **Settings menu**.
2. Find **Apps** on the sidebar and click on it.
3. Find **Default applications** and click on them.
4. Type **"Chrome"** into the search field and then choose it when it appears.
5. A **Set default button** will appear at the top of the page.
6. Once you click **Set default**, all file and link types will convert to Chrome as the default browser.

The method takes just a second but will save a great deal of time in the future. Whenever you open a file type linked with a web browser, Windows 11 should launch your new default browser, Google Chrome.

How To Download And Install Any Software Onto Your Windows 11 Computer

You can use an internet browser like Google chrome to locate and download any software you want to install on your PC. This can include antivirus software, browsers, VPN (virtual private network) services, office, and productivity programs, media players, photo and video editors, PC repair tools, email clients, backup and recovery assistants, file management systems, and social programs.

You can find the software you are looking for by typing in the name and 'download' into your browser search bar. Make sure to click the link that takes you to the software developer's own trusted website. You must purchase many programs before downloading and installing them, including Microsoft Office 365 and various Adobe products. As soon as you have fulfilled the payment process, you will be redirected to a download link with steps detailing how to install the software properly.

Ensure that your computer meets the minimum system requirements for the software you want to download. This information is available on the website. Next, find the download link and accept any required terms and conditions. When the file is downloaded, you can begin the installation process. Most programs will come with installation guides to assist you, and you will only need to check some boxes and click Next, Accept, or Install.

How To Install VLC Media Player

Viewing videos, movies, and short films on a desktop or laptop display is entertaining. However, the video player must be of high quality so that you can easily access the many capabilities. We'll begin by downloading the most recent version of the VLC media player. You will be taken to the official VLC media player downloads website when you find the right link on the internet.

Install VLC Media Player on Microsoft Windows 11

- Once the download is complete, open the **".exe" file** for the VLC media player in the location where it was downloaded. To launch the installation window, double-click the downloaded file.
- In the installation box, you must first pick the installation language for the VLC media player. Simply click the **Ok** button to accept the default English language.
- Click the **Next button** on the Welcome screen during VLC media player installation.
- In the installation window, you'll be prompted to accept the licensing agreement. Click the **Next button** to accept the License Agreement.
- In the Choose Components box, no more components need to be installed. Therefore, click the Next button again.
- Select the installation folder for the VLC media player at this point. We will not make any changes here, so just click the **Install button**.
- Click the **Complete button** after the installation is complete, and congratulations, you have successfully installed the VLC media player on your Windows 11 laptop or desktop.

How To Install An Antivirus

If you're having issues with your computer, it is important that you keep a virus scanner installed on your PC.

If you click on 'Internet Security under the 'Control Panel' menu, you can download a free security solution.

Microsoft also offers a security essential tool for Windows 7 and Windows 8 users.

You can choose to download the entire suite of Microsoft Security Essentials applications, or you can download the suite of Windows Essentials applications only.

To run Microsoft Security Essentials, click on 'Security Essentials' under the 'Control Panel' menu, and then click on 'Search' to search for the free app.

When the search is complete, you can download the app. The tool can be used to scan your computer, detect viruses, and help you identify problems.

How To Install WhatsApp Messenger

WhatsApp is a messaging application that enables you to transmit voice memos, photos, videos, and other information. It provides a convenient platform for communication with family and friends. However, if you want to use WhatsApp on your computer, WhatsApp Desktop for Windows is an excellent alternative. It is an extension of your WhatsApp account on your PC.

In addition to transmitting images, voice conversations, and documents, it adds location sharing, encrypted communications, video calls, and business profiles to the list.

Download WhatsApp for Windows 11 from the Microsoft Store

The Microsoft Store offers the official WhatsApp Desktop client for Windows PCs. To learn how to accomplish it, please follow these steps:

- To begin, open the **Start** menu and search **"Store."** To access the Microsoft Store, click on its result in the search results.
- Next, search for **"WhatsApp"** in the Microsoft Store and pick **"WhatsApp Desktop"** from the search results.
- Click **"Get"** to download and install WhatsApp Desktop on your Windows-based computer.
- You should be able to use the application immediately after installing it on your computer.

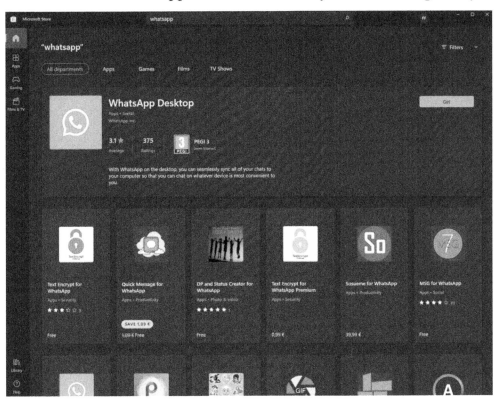

Install WhatsApp on Windows 11 from the Official Website

In addition to the Microsoft Store, the WhatsApp Desktop program may be downloaded and used on Windows 11 from WhatsApp's official website. To learn how to accomplish it, follow the instructions below:

- Launch your web browser and go to **whatsapp.com/download**.

- Click **"DOWNLOAD FOR WINDOWS"** to download WhatsApp to your Windows 11 computer.
- After the download is complete, execute the **"WhatsAppSetup.exe" file**, and after the installation, you will be presented with a welcome screen and instructions for using WhatsApp on Windows.

How To Install Zoom

Zoom is most people's preferred video conferencing software that enables many distant employees to communicate with coworkers through video and audio conferences. You must meet certain conditions if you want to download and install zoom on Windows 11.

A PC with speakers and a microphone is required. Webcams are suggested but not mandatory. If you have a Windows 11 computer with speakers, a microphone, and a camera, read on to discover how to download and install the Zoom software.

Installing the Zoom app on Windows 11

Before your Zoom conference begins, you must download and install the Zoom program to guarantee a positive experience.

- To download Zoom, visit the following link: https://zoom.us/ download
- Click the Download button under **"Zoom Client for Meetings"** in the Download Center.

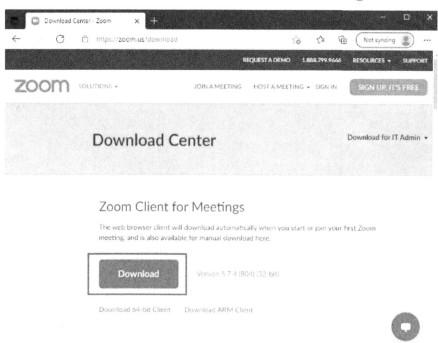

- Once the file is downloaded, click the **Open file link**.
- Alternatively, go to the Downloads folder and double-click the downloaded file to start the installation.
- When the following screen asks whether Zoom may make modifications to your computer during installation, choose **Yes**.

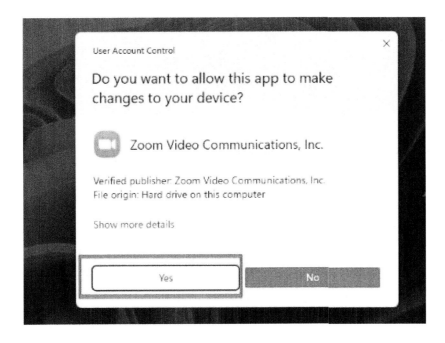

- The Zoom app should then be installed, and you should be able to sign in or join a meeting.
- Simply choose to **Join a Meeting** if you do not already have an account.
- Then, enter the details of the meeting and click **Join**.

Chapter 6:
Windows File Explorer

Windows File Structure

When working with folders, most users don't fully understand working with files. For example, let's say you want to create a new folder, and if you click on new, you can choose to create a new shortcut, a new folder, or a new bunch of other things if you create just a new folder. So, click on new and then choose folder. Then you have to name the folder, and then you hit enter.

Changing File And Folder Views

In Windows 11 you can easily switch between different types of views using the View button in the Command bar. You can choose to view extra large icons, large icons, medium icons, small icons, lists, details, tiles or content. You can also switch to "Compact view" which minimizes the amount of space between files and folders. This feature has been included because Windows 11 is optimized for touch-enabled devices where larger spaces between different files, folders and icons make selecting them easier when using your finger. However, this feature can easily be enabled or disabled to suit your needs.

In the View menu, you can also decide what kind of information you want, including a navigation pane, a details pane, a preview pane, item checkboxes, file name extensions and hidden items. The Navigation pane appears on the left side of the window. It provides shortcuts to some of the parent libraries on your computer, including the "Quick Access" library, 'OneDrive,' "This PC," and your 'Network.' Within "Quick Access" you can find the Desktop, Downloads, Documents, Pictures, Music and Videos. You can choose to show or hide the Navigation Pane entirely.

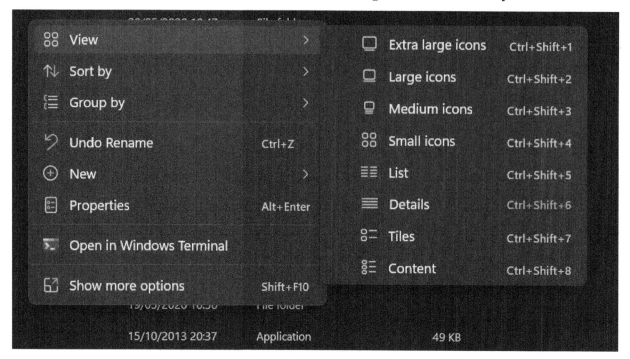

The Details Pane and Preview Pane work similarly to the Navigation pane though they will show up on the right side of the File Explorer Window. These panes will show you the file or folder you selected. The Details Pane shows the name, file format, last date modified, size, and date your selected folder or file was created. As the name suggests, the Preview Pane will show you a preview of the selected file. You can scroll through the preview to see different pages in the document using this feature.

The "Item check boxes" feature is a new feature to Windows 11 implemented with touch-screens in mind. It allows you to select multiple files or folders so that you can move, copy, paste or cut them. By clicking this button, you will see small check boxes appear over all the items in your File Explorer, which can be checked or unchecked. This feature works exactly the same way as holding down the Ctrl button while using your mouse to click on multiple items.

Windows 11 also allows you to show or hide the file extensions in the File Explorer. The file extensions reveal the file format, which lets Windows know what kind of file it is dealing with and which application is needed to open and work or run the file. File extensions are three or four letters long, usually found right at the end of a file's name. They include JPEG, JPG, PNG, DOC, DOCX, XLS, PPT, or ZIP, though many others exist.

Finally you can also choose to view or hide "Hidden items" using the View Menu. Windows offers the ability to hide certain files and folders, and many are hidden by default, because these are not meant to be modified. They often include important system-related data, though any file can be hidden. You can toggle this feature to show or hide these files using the "Hidden items" button.

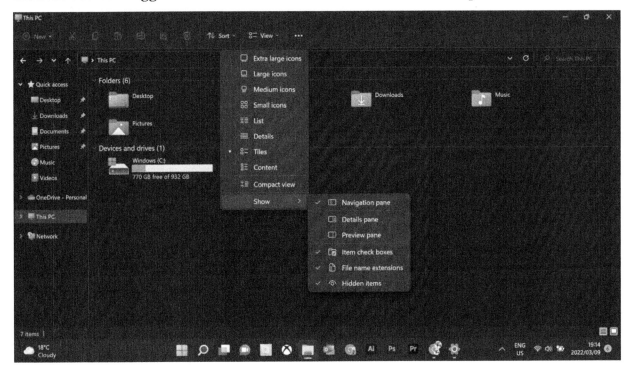

Moving, Copying, Renaming And Deleting Files
Moving and Copying and Pasting Files and Folders
Copying or moving files or folders is what you can't do without any stress. Let me make it simple by showing you the two best ways of moving or copying a file:

Right-Clicking Method

1. Right-click the source file or folder you want to move or copy and select Cut or Copy depending on whether you are moving or copying.

2. Move to the destination folder and right-click it, then select paste from the fly-out list to paste the cut or copy item.

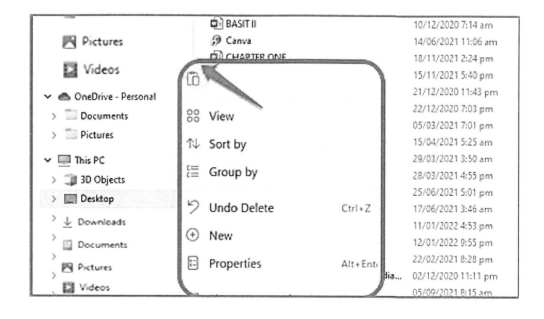

Drag and Drop Method

1. Open **File Explorer Windows** twice and place them beside each other.

2. Place the mouse on the file or folder you want to move or copy from the source Windows and hold down the right mouse button.

3. Then **drag the file** to the **destination folder** in the destination Windows, release the right mouse button as soon as you reach the destination folder, and select **Move or Copy** from the pop-up list depending on the action you want to carry out.

Note: it's necessary you hold down the right mouse button; if you hold the left mouse button, Windows will be confused about the action you want to initiate.

Deleting Files and Folders

Deleting files and folders is pretty straightforward, and all you have to do is highlight the file or folder and click the *Trash Can* button on the toolbar. Or you can right-click a file and choose Show more options -> Delete or press the Delete key on your keyboard. By default, Windows will send the file or folder to the Recycle Bin rather than delete them permanently.

Depending on your Recycle Bin settings, you may or may not get a confirmation prompt asking you to confirm that you want to send the file or folder to the Recycle Bin. It will also provide details about the file's size and the date it was modified.

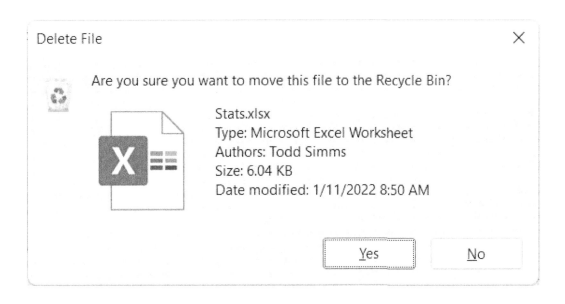

If you made a mistake and want the file back, you can use the Ctrl-Z keyboard shortcut to *undo* the action and have the file undeleted from the Recycle Bin and returned to its original location. Keep in mind that Ctrl-Z only works for the last operation performed, so if you've deleted another file since the one you wanted to be recovered, it won't work, and you will have to go into the Recycle Bin to get it back.

Renaming Files and Folders

Don't worry about any file or folder name that sounds somehow to you. You can do away with an offensive file or folder name by changing such a name. How do I change a file or folder name? Let me show you how:

- Right-click the **file or folder name** you want to change and pick **Rename** from the fly-out menu or the File Explorer menu.

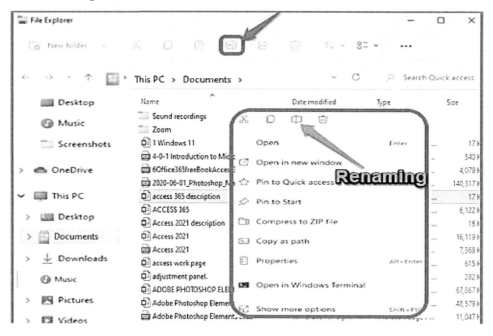

- The previous name will be highlighted, begin to enter a new name, and the previous name will be erased.
- Strike Enter key when you are done typing the name or click an empty area within the File Explorer to authenticate the process.

Put the following note to memory before changing any file or folder name:

1. Don't try renaming your 6 Main folders' names **(Desktop, Documents, Downloads, Pictures, Music, and Photos)**. Renaming them can disrupt the activities of your PC and cause serious damage to your Windows.

2. Note that **renaming a file or folder name** doesn't change anything from the content of the concerned file or folder. The content of the file or folder remains the same. The only change is the file or folder name.

3. Don't bother **renaming any opening files or folders** because Windows will permit no alteration on the opening folder until you close such a file or folder.

Creating A New Folder Or File

Creating a new folder in File Explorer is easier than ever. You simply need to click the 'New' button on the Command Bar's left side. This will present you with a drop-down menu giving you the option to create either a new folder or shortcut. This menu will also allow you to create a range of new files, including Microsoft Word documents, Microsoft Excel spreadsheets or Microsoft PowerPoint presentations. This action will open up the relevant program so that you can begin working on the new document.

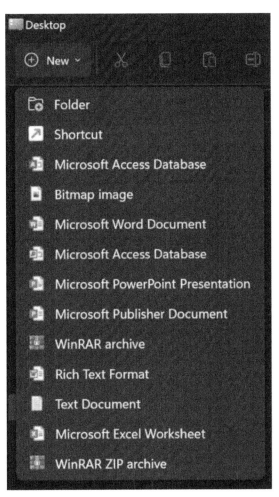

How To Delete A File Or Folder

You can delete a folder or file in File Explorer by selecting it and then pressing the 'Delete' button in the Command Bar. You can also right-click on any files or folders you want to delete which will bring up a small menu where you will also find an option to 'delete.'

Default Windows Folders

The folder for Windows 11 is a specific directory assigned by the operating system, where a user stores his personal files independently.

Currently, the folder user has several folders among which we find:

- Documents
- Music
- Videos and
- Downloads.

Searching For Files And Folders

File Explorer makes it easy to find a file or folder no matter where it is stored on your computer. Below the Command bar, you will see an Address bar on the left and a Search bar on the right. All you need to do is type the name of the file or folder that you are looking for into this search bar. Your search results will be displayed in the File Explorer window.

How To Undo Or Redo An Action

If you accidentally delete a file or move something to a location by mistake, you can easily undo this action using your keyboard shortcuts. Simply press Ctrl+Z to undo an action and Ctrl+Y to redo it.

How To Recover A Deleted File Folder

One of the key components of the desktop is access to the recycle bin. So typically, when you delete something from your computer, it will automatically be put in a recycled bin. So if you want to retrieve something from a recycle bin, you can double click the recycle bin, which will display what you have recently deleted. Then right-click on it and choose to restore it.

Chapter 7:
How To Navigate on The Web With Windows 11

Introducing Microsoft Edge

Microsoft Edge, a built-in web browser for Windows 11, is one of the best web browsers available to surf the internet. It presents an improvement over internet explorer and has several features for enhanced productivity. Some of the immense benefits of browsing with the Microsoft Edge browser are minimum power usage and safe and fast internet access.

To open the edge browser;

Go to Start > Microsoft Edge

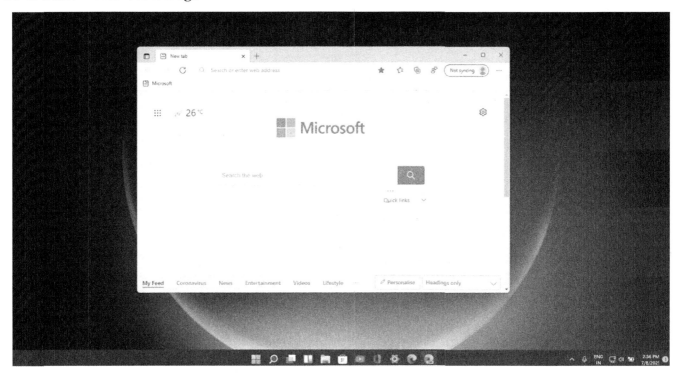

Using Multiple Tabs

You can open many tabs at once on the Edge browser. You can navigate different opened web pages by clicking the tabs above the window of these web pages. Please see the screenshot under Get to know the Edge Browser Interface for a pictorial view of Edge browser tabs.

You can use the following keyboard shortcuts to manage tabs:

- Ctrl + T: Open a new tab
- Ctrl + W: Close a tab
- Ctrl + Tab: switch from one tab to the next
- Ctrl + K: Open a new duplicate tab of the tab you are presently viewing
- In addition, you can move straight to a tab by pressing Ctrl and the number of the tab. For example, to move to the fourth tab, press Ctrl + 4

- To open a link in a separate tab, press Ctrl and that link.

Using Favorites

With several billions of web pages in the internet world, you just have to select your favorites. Like any other modern-day browsers, Microsoft Edge allows you to select a favorite or bookmark a page. This makes it easier to visit the website or webpage in the future.

1. Tap on the "**Add this page to Favorite**" icon at the right edge of the address bar to access the favorite added box.

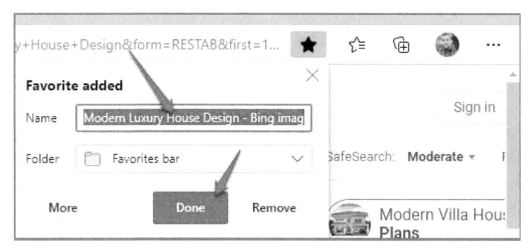

2. You can use the same name or edit it to your desired name and click on the **Done** button to add the page to the favorite list.

Note: when it is time to check your favorite place you've visited before, you will need to click on the favorite list icon to access the list of all the favorite sites you've added. Click on the actual one you want to visit to see that amazing content once again.

Perhaps, the time has gone over the previous favorite site you've added to the favorite list, no qualm. You can send it out of the favorite list anytime you see that a certain list is no more interesting to you by right-clicking the offending site's name and selecting **Delete** from the fly-out list.

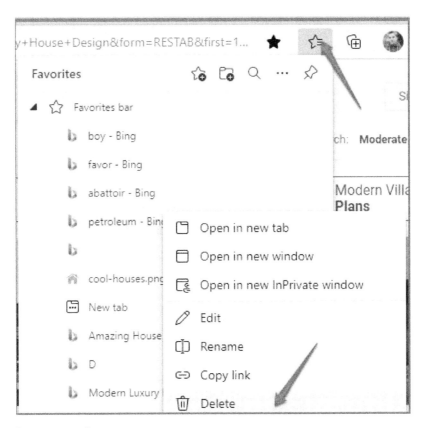

Customizing Edge Settings

Edge once again boasts of being an advanced channel and presents a feature that fans of customization will surely like. The possibility allows the establishment of personalized images in the browser.

It is now possible to customize Edge with game backgrounds, thanks to the Xbox New Tab extension. A function that can be accessed if you have an Edge version equal to or greater than 83.0.471.0. We can choose our favorite image as the background of the "New tab" page by just following a series of steps;

- Once inside Edge, we go to the "Tab Settings" menu thanks to the gear icon, and within it we mark the "Custom" field where we will select "Your own image" in the background option.
- At that point, you will only have to choose which image you want to use as a background.

How To Add A Bookmark

A bookmark is a way to save and store a website's URL so you can return to it in the future.

Microsoft Edge:

- Visit the website URL you want to save.
- Click the Star button on the right-hand side of the toolbar.
- Click the Star button with the + sign to add a 'Favorite.'
- You will see the name of your website appear.
- Hit Enter to save.
- You can customize the website's name or add folders and subfolders to keep your Favorites organized.
- You can also use the keyboard shortcut Ctrl + D to quickly add a website to your Favorites.

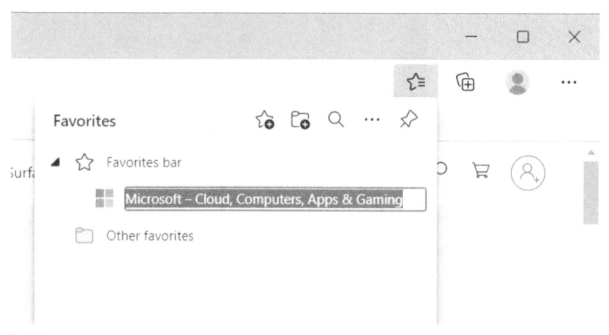

Google Chrome

- Visit the website URL you want to save.
- Click the Star button on the right-hand side of the toolbar.
- You will see the name of your website appear and the folder.
- Hit Enter to save.
- You can customize the website's name or add folders and subfolders to keep your Bookmarks organized.
- You can also use the keyboard shortcut Ctrl + D to quickly add a website to your Bookmarks.

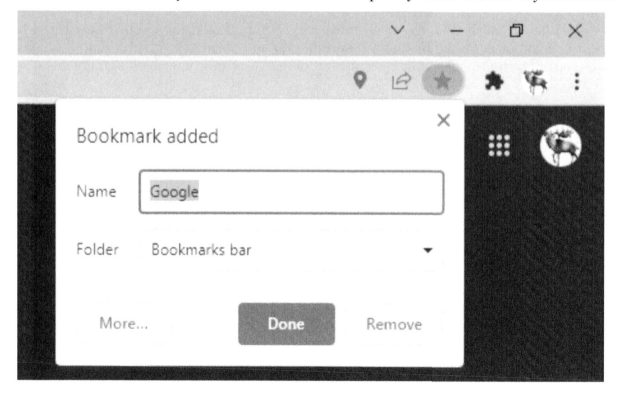

How To Show The Bookmarks Bar

You can display your bookmarks and bookmark folders in a bar at the top of your browser.

Microsoft Edge

- Click the Tools button, select Settings > Appearance > Customize the toolbar > Show favorites bar.
- Select 'Always' or "Only on new tabs" to display the favorites bar.
- You can also use the keyboard shortcut Ctrl + Shift + B to quickly hide or show the Favorites bar.

Google Chrome

- Click the Tools button, and select Settings > Appearance > Show bookmarks bar.
- Toggle this to display the bookmarks bar.
- You can also use the keyboard shortcut Ctrl + Shift + B to quickly hide or show the bookmarks bar.

How To Set A New Homepage

When you open your browser, it will direct you to a default homepage, or you can set your own homepage as any website.

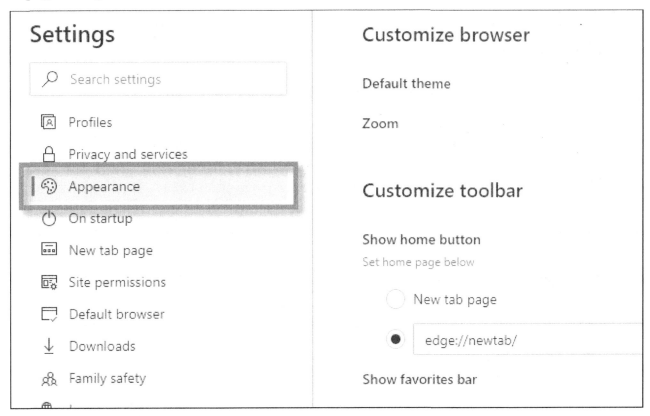

Microsoft Edge

- Go to Settings > Appearance > Customize toolbar.
- Toggle the "Home button" option and click "Set button URL."

- This will direct you to the homepage settings, where you can set your homepage button to refer you to a new tab or a specific URL.

Google Chrome

- Go to Settings > Appearance.
- Toggle the button for "Show Home button" to 'on.'
- Choose whether to set your homepage to a New Tab Page or a specific URL.

View And Delete Your Browsing History

Edge browser collects the history of the web pages you visit and stores it.

You can manage Microsoft Edge browsing history in many ways, but some ways are smarter than others.

Microsoft Edge

- Click the Tools button, then select History.
- You will see some of the web pages you have visited in the last 90 days in a small window.
- You can delete individual records by hovering over them and clicking the X that appears on the right-hand side.
- To clear all your browsing history, click on the three horizontal dots at the top of the History window and select "Clear browsing data."

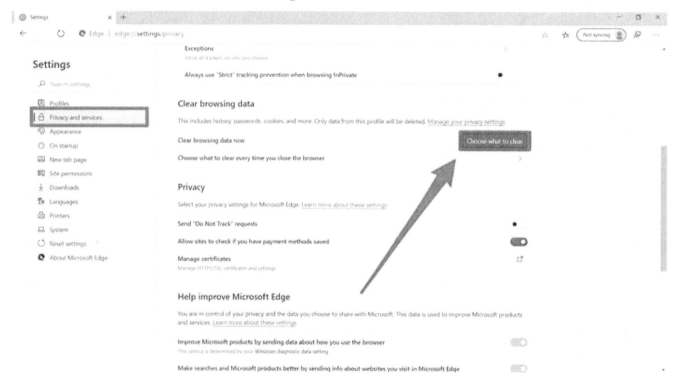

- You can also open your browser history by pressing Ctrl+H.
- To see more detailed information, such as the date and time you visited your web pages, select "Open history page" after clicking the three horizontal dots at the top of the History window.

Google Chrome

- Click the Tools button, then select History.

- You will see some of the web pages you have visited in the last 90 days in a small window.
- You can open one of these pages by clicking on it.
- To delete your search history, open the History tab or press Ctrl+H.
- You can select and deselect individual records using the checkboxes and then press the Delete button in the top right corner.
- You can delete all your browser history using the "Clear browsing data" button on the left side of the page.

How To Enable Private Browsing

Sometimes, you will not want your browser to save any information about your visit to a webpage. For instance, if you don't want a website to save cookies on your device or you don't want your child to know you are browsing about favorite gifts to buy for them.

In addition, InPrivate mode browsing allows for multiple sessions. For example, you may access your Yahoo mail account (or another web account) on a normal window and use the secret mode tab to open the Yahoo mail account of that of your friend or family member without logging out of your own account. Pages viewed in secret mode are not listed in your browser history or search history and leave no traces (such as cookies) on your device.

Microsoft Edge - InPrivate browsing

- To activate InPrivate browsing, click the More actions (...) button and select New InPrivate window.
- You can also open an InPrivate window using the keyboard shortcut Ctrl+ Shift+ N.

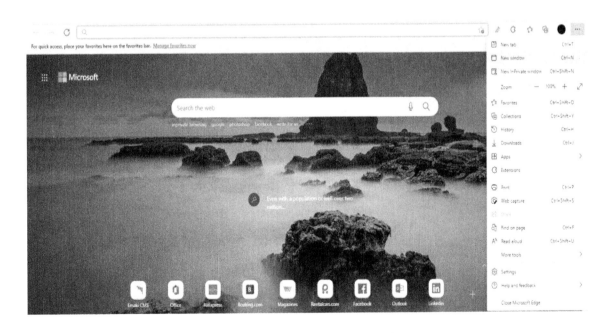

Google Chrome - Incognito Mode

- To open a new tab using Incognito mode, click on the three vertical dots in the top right of your window.
- Click "New Incognito window."
- Also, you can open an Incognito window using the keyboard shortcut Ctrl + Shift + N.

How To Zoom In On A Page

Microsoft Edge

To zoom a webpage in Microsoft Edge, press Ctrl and + key to zoom in and press Ctrl and - key to zoom out. Alternatively, open the More actions (...) tab and click on plus or minus sign next Zoom.

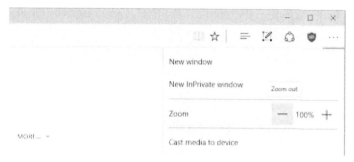

Google Chrome

- Click on the three vertical dots in the top right of your browser window.
- Navigate to 'Zoom' and press + or - to zoom in or out.
- Also, you can hold the Ctrl button while using the wheel on your mouse to zoom in or out.

How To Block Ads

Many websites display intrusive and distracting ads that pop up in your browser. You can use your internet browser to block some of these ads.

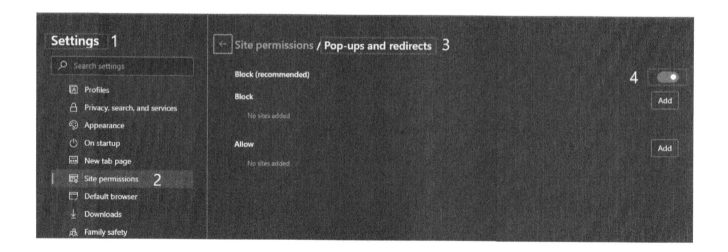

Microsoft Edge

- Click on the Tools button, then select Settings > Cookies and site permissions > Pop-ups and redirects.
- Make sure to turn this setting on.
- You can also customize these settings and add or block certain websites from showing pop-ups or redirecting you to another page.

Google Chrome

- Click on the Tools Button, then select Settings > Security and Privacy > Site settings > Pop-ups and redirects.
- Under "Default behavior," ensure that you select the "Don't allow sites to send pop-ups or use redirects" option.
- Also, you can customize these settings to allow pop-ups from specific websites or ban pop-ups from certain websites by inputting their URLs.

How To Download A File

You may want to download content such as a document or an image when browsing the web.

1. Open the webpage.

2. Locate and click on the download link.

3. Click Save.

4. Wait for the download to finish and click on Open.

Please note that if you are downloading a pdf document, it will automatically open with the Edge browser pdf reader.

You can pause a download by clicking on Pause while the file is still downloading. Please note that the file will still need to be downloaded to use this option. If the file has already been downloaded completely, the Pause button will not be available.

⊡	Open image in new tab	
⊡	Save image as	
⊡	Copy image	
	Copy image link	
	Create QR Code for this image	
⊡	Search the web for image	
⊡	Search Bing in sidebar for image	
⊡	Open in Immersive Reader	F9
⊡	Add to Collections	>
⊡	Share	
⊡	Web select	Ctrl+Shift+X
⊡	Web capture	Ctrl+Shift+S
⊡	Inspect	

Add-Ons And Extension

Microsoft Edge

Edge has had extensions for quite some time, but in the Creators Update, Edge got a complete makeover.

The main thing that's changed is the look and feel of the browser. To access extensions, click on the three dots in the lower-left corner of the browser. Click on Extensions, and then select Browse New. You'll see a list of extension categories like News & Weather, Finance, Sports, Entertainment, etc.

Click on an extension and it will be installed. To remove an extension, click on the three dots in the lower-left corner of the browser, and then click Remove.

Google Chrome

- You can find extensions for Chrome at chrome.google.com/webstore/category/extensions. You can manage your existing extensions by clicking Tools > More tools > Extensions.
- The link will take you to the Google Web Store, where you can browse through thousands of extensions for different purposes, including accessibility, blogging, developer tools, fun, news & weather, photos, productivity, search tools, shopping, and social and communication, and sports. The Web Store will also show you some featured apps in different categories such as Recommended for you, Favorites of 2021, Extensions starter kit, Travel smarter, and more.
- To install an extension, click on it, select "Add to Chrome," then select Add Extension on the pop-up window.
- You should now see a new icon next to your address bar, which you can click on to access the extension's features.
- If you do not see a new icon, you should see an icon of a puzzle piece which you can click to show all of your extensions. You can use the pin buttons to pin or unpin the extension icons to your taskbar so you can always see them.

Chapter 8:
Windows 11 Settings

Windows 11 Settings App

The Windows Settings application is a new feature that allows you to view and make changes to computer settings such as uninstalling applications, setting power options, viewing hard drive space, and accessing Ease of Access/Accessibility options. To access the Windows Settings page:

- Click the Start button.
- Click the Settings icon.

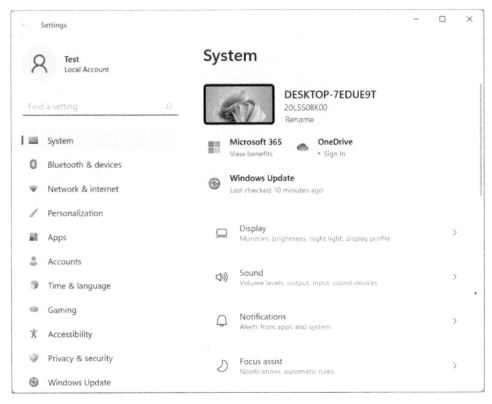

It includes the following;

1. System

2. Bluetooth and Devices

3. Network and Internet

4. Personalization

5. Apps

6. Accounts

7. Time and Language

8. Gaming

9. Accessibility

10. Privacy and Security

11. Windows Update

System Settings

The settings covered here include the ones related to the orientation of the display, sound settings, resolution, and so on. These categories are known as the sub-divisions of the system settings.

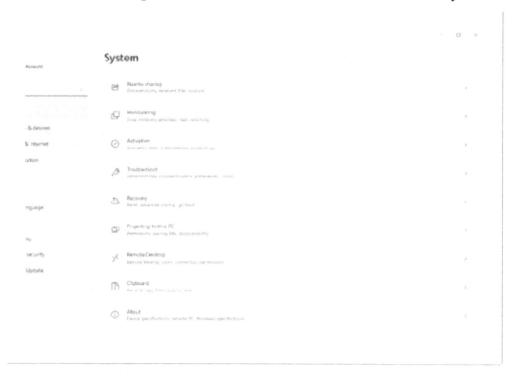

1. <u>Display</u>: From here, you get to do the following;

- Alter the brightness of your device's display
- Application of warm colors to the display screen by fixing the required duration for the night light.
- Adjustment of screen resolution
- Adjustment of the screen orientation
- Change of the default graphics settings

2. <u>Sound</u>: This feature allows you to do the following;

- Adjust the volume of the system
- Pair a new input device
- Set an input volume to whatever you prefer
- To troubleshoot whatever issues you have with sounds.

3. <u>Notifications</u>: Here, you get to do any of the following;

- Turn on notifications and alerts from applications
- Turn off notifications and alerts from applications
- Turn on/off notifications from your contacts

102

- Turn on/off notifications from your system.

4. <u>Focus Assist</u>: This feature allows you to do the following;

- Choose the notifications you want to receive
- Check the notifications you missed
- Summary of details you missed when the Focus Assist was enabled

5. <u>Power</u>: This feature allows you to;

- Adjust settings connected to Sleep
- Adjust settings connected to Battery Usage
- Adjust settings related to Battery Saving

6. <u>Storage</u>: This feature allows you to;

- Adjust settings related to Storage spaces
- Adjust settings related to Backup options
- Adjust settings related to Cleanup offers
- Adjust settings related to Configuration tips.

7. <u>Nearby Sharing</u>: This feature allows you to;

- Share files
- Share photos
- Share links with other proximal Window devices.

8. <u>Multitasking</u>: This feature allows you to;

- Resize and rearrange the Window screens on your device
- Practice the process of switching tasks.

9. <u>Activation</u>: This feature covers the following sections;

- Product key
- Activation states
- Subscriptions

10. <u>Troubleshoot</u>: This feature allows you to adjust features related to the following;

- Internet Connections
- Windows Update
- Printer
- Audio
- Bluetooth

The feature also allows you to see the kind of troubleshooting your computer has previously run. Troubleshooting your device will help you fix several of the problems you could have with the Windows 11 O.S.

11. <u>Recovery</u>: This feature helps you fix any issue with your device. If you do not get a solution after working with the Troubleshooting step, you could use the 'Reset' option and have your Windows reinstalled. The Recovery feature also comprises an Advanced Startup option,

which helps to restart your P.C. Usually, the restarting is done with the aid of a USB drive or disc.

12. Projecting to this P.C: This feature allows you to alter things that have to do with the different permissions associated with your P.C. When you want to work with the feature for 'Screen Mirroring,' you get to project your P.C. to the screen you are working with at that moment. That way, the keyboard, mouse, and other connected devices are in sync.

13. Remote Desktop: This feature secures a connection to your P.C. so that you can control it using another proximal device. By enabling this feature, any of the chosen user accounts could connect to your P.C. locally.

14. Clipboard: This feature allows you to run functions like the ones listed out below;

- Cut
- Copy
- Sync
- Clear clipboard settings

15. About: This feature allows you to do the following;

- Get details as regards your P.C.
- Know the name of your device
- Get the I.D. of your device
- Get the Product ID of your device
- Product key activation
- Remote Desktop
- Device Manager
- BitLocker
- Get the Installed RAM
- Know the system type
- Know the Windows O.S. specifications
- Get suitable support for your P.C.

Bluetooth & Devices

Windows 11 allows users to connect computer paraphernalia, such as a mouse, keyboard, headphones, speakers, microphones, and other devices via Bluetooth connectivity. Connecting devices to your Windows 11 computer via Bluetooth is straightforward and easy.

Enabling Bluetooth Connectivity in Your Windows 11 Computer
Whether your computer's Bluetooth functionality is enabled or not will depend on how Windows 11 was installed on your PC. You can easily turn the Bluetooth functionality on or off via the Action Center or even the Settings menu.

Turning the Bluetooth On via Settings Menu

To enable or disable your PC's Bluetooth via the Settings menu, click **Start** and select **Settings**. In the Settings window, click **Bluetooth & Devices**. Next, scroll down to the **Bluetooth switch** option and toggle it on or off.

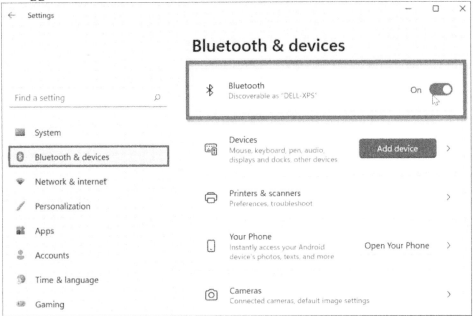

Turning the Bluetooth On via Action Center

To check the status of your PC's Bluetooth, press the **Windows key + A** on your keyboard. This will open the Action Center window. Next, click the **Bluetooth** icon to enable it if it is disabled. Otherwise, leave it as it is.

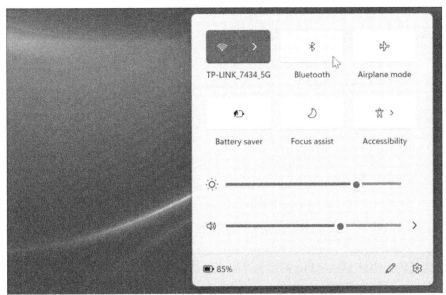

How to Pair Bluetooth Devices to your Windows 11 Computer

When your PC's Bluetooth functionality is on, you can connect it to any Bluetooth-enabled device, whether a phone, tablet or speakers. To pair your Windows 11 PC with a specific device, make sure the device is within range of your computer. At the same time, ensure that the device is discoverable by turning on its "pairing mode."

To connect the device to your PC via Bluetooth, click **Start** and open **Settings**. On the Settings page, select **Bluetooth & Devices** and click **Add Device**. When you click the **Bluetooth** option at the top, your Windows 11 PC will start scanning for nearby devices. When the device you wish to connect appears on your computer screen, click on it to begin pairing.

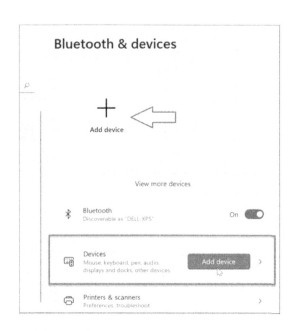

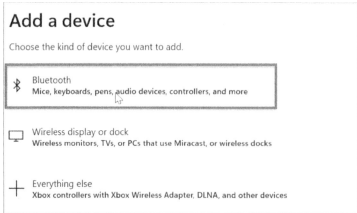

Once the connection has been established, you will receive a prompt informing you that the pairing is successful. You can then start using your Bluetooth device with your Windows 11 computer.

Disconnecting or Removing a Bluetooth Device from Your Windows 11 PC
Go to Start and access Settings to remove or disconnect a Bluetooth device from your Windows 11 PC. From there, click **Bluetooth & Devices** and find the device you wish to remove. Once you've confirmed the device you want to disconnect, click on the three dots icon in the upper right corner and click **Disconnect**. This will unpair the device but will keep its name listed so you can connect to it again in the future.

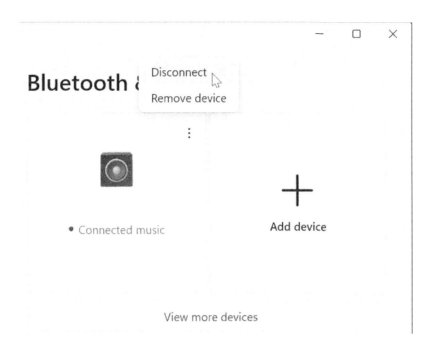

If you wish to use the same device again, just click **Connect**.

If you want to remove the device permanently, click **Remove Device** instead and click **Yes** to confirm.

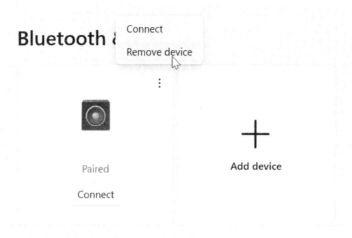

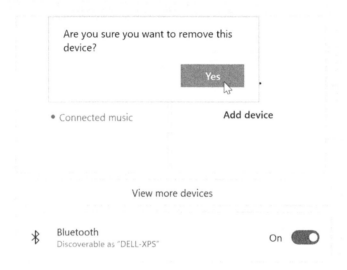

How to Use the Bluetooth Device Wizard

Windows 11 allows you to use the Bluetooth Device Wizard to add Bluetooth devices to your computer. We are unsure whether they will still be available in the future, but they are still usable as of this writing.

To connect your device to your PC via the Device Wizard, ensure that your device is in pairing mode and is discoverable. On your PC, go to **Start** and type "device pairing wizard." Click the Device Wizard icon from the search results. This will open the classic pairing wizard.

Next, search for **Bluetooth devices** and select the device you wish to pair. Click **Next**.

A progress bar will appear, indicating that your computer is establishing a connection with the device.

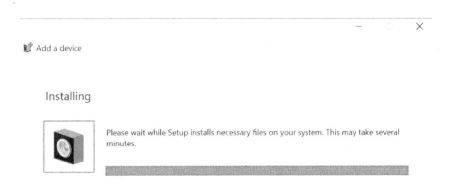

Once your device is connected, its name will appear in **Device and Printers** in the Control **Panel**. Should you want to disconnect or completely remove the device via the classic Control Panel, right-click on the device name in **Device and Printers** and click **Remove Device** on the window that appears. Click **Yes** to confirm your action.

Network & Internet

The Network & Internet Settings provide settings related to connecting to networks, usually for accessing the internet. They include:

- Wi-Fi: This contains options for connecting to the internet via your Wi-Fi router (or public hotspots if you are away from home). There is also an option for managing your Wi-Fi networks.
- Ethernet: This can be used if you are connecting to the internet with an Ethernet cable (RJ45). This connects to the internet port on your computer and internet access is delivered using your telephone line via the service provider's router.

- <u>VPN</u>: This can be used to connect to a corporate network over VPN (Virtual Private Network).If you are doing this, you will need to contain settings from your network administrator.
- <u>Mobile Hotspot</u>: This feature permits sharing your device's internet connection with another device. The sharing usually occurs via Bluetooth or Wi-Fi.
- <u>Airplane mode</u>: This can be used to turn off wireless communication when you are on a plane, so you can still use your laptop safely.
- <u>Proxy</u>: This contains options for using a proxy server for Ethernet or Wi-Fi connection.
- <u>Dial-up</u>: This can be used if you have a dial-up modem for connecting to the internet. This is not common these days but is still a valid means of internet access.
- <u>Advanced network settings</u>: This feature allows you to manage features like Network Adapters, Bluetooth connection, Ethernet, WI-FI, Data consumption, Hardware and connection issues, etc.

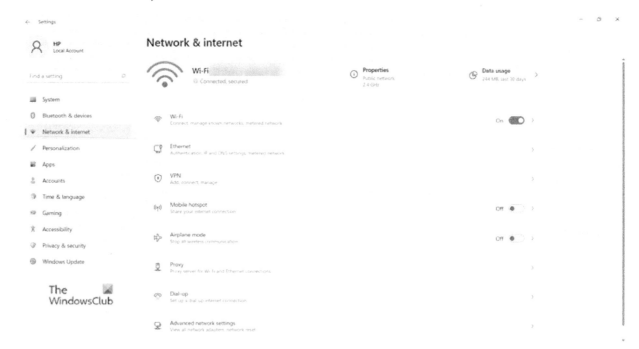

Personalization

Personalization helps you customize the look of your computer to look exactly the way you want. It helps you change the complete appearance of your PC, including the color, background, lock screen, and others to ensure your PC look, behave, and reflect the way you want it.

Without much ado, let's move to the Personalization category and tweak the look of your PC by:

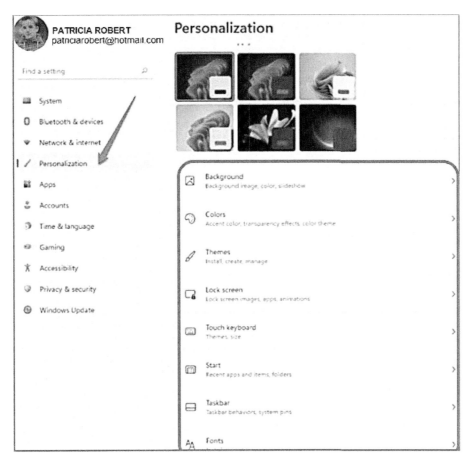

Navigating to Settings Panel and tap on Personalization to access all the settings you can use to tweak the appearance of your PC on the right side as it is described below:

1. **Background:** An option to tweak the color or photo of your desktop screen, some users call it wallpaper.

2. **Color:** This is used to select the color you will use to frame your background, taskbar, start menu, and Windows app simply by selecting a color from the color gallery.

3. **Themes:** This helps you to save your color, background, and lock screen settings as a theme so that you can quickly pick the settings next time your background, color, and lock screen as a whole. You can also navigate to the Microsoft Store app and click on Get More themes to download innumerable themes.

4. **Lock screen**: You can click on this to choose the photo you want to be seen immediately you switch ON your computer; though Windows automatically place a photo into your lock screen, you can change it if you desire.

5. **Touch Keyboard**: This lets you choose various colors for a different area on the onscreen keyboard for the onscreen user and change the size of the onscreen keyboard.

6. **Start**: It helps you customize your start menu.

7. **Taskba**r: It helps to customize the look and arrangements of your taskbar.

8. **Fonts**: This is used to get more font types downloaded to your PC by moving to Microsoft Store and clicking on Get More fonts to access the available online fonts.

9. **Device Usage**: It shows you the pattern of your PC usage concerning gaming, school, entertainment, and more.

Apps

This feature allows you to control the following features;

- Apps and features: Here, you get to see a list of all the applications on your device and other settings that are in sync.
- Default apps: This feature allows you to set defaults for apps.
- Offline maps: This feature lets you download map applications. Those apps usually come out to be very useful when you do not have a connection to the internet. You also get to update your maps if you wish.
- Optional features: This feature allows you to merge features like fonts and tools into the list of existing features.
- Apps for websites: This feature allows you to create links to websites that can be used in place of browsers.
- Video playback: This feature allows you to manage features related to HDR streaming and other battery features.
- Startup: This feature allows for the configuration of applications to begin to run when you sign in and log out of them.

Accounts

This feature allows you to control features related to the following sub-divisions;

- Your Info: Here, you get to manage settings related to your account. From here, you can get to sign in to your Microsoft account.
- Email and accounts: Here, you get to manage the accounts related to your email, calendar, and contacts. You can also merge accounts related to your work, school, or other Microsoft content.
- Sign-in: This feature allows you to manage features related to facial recognition, fingerprint, PIN, password, security key, and other forms of password. The Dynamic lock feature also allows you to lock your device even when you aren't in close range.
- Family and other users: This feature allows you to ensure that your family members have a nice experience with the internet. You get to control what they have access to easily, and so on.
- Windows Backup: This feature allows you to keep your files safe, so, in a case where you lose your device, you can easily get your details restored.
- Access work or school: This feature allows you to link up with any account you have at work or school.

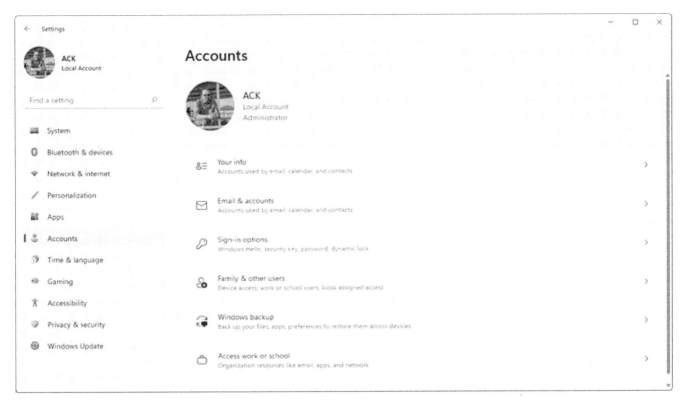

Time & Language

This feature gives you the privilege to change the time zone if it is different from where you are coming from and also allows you to change your PC location and language with the location and language of the place you are currently. To modify your time, date, language, location, and others, kindly find your way to the Settings Panel and click on Time and Date category to access the list of settings you can tweak as listed below:

- **Date and Time:** This can be used to adjust your PC time and date. it leads you to the same route when you click the time and date icon on the taskbar.
- **Language and Region:** Here, you can change the language and location of your PC to the new region you've just moved to.
- **Typing:** Thus feature allows you to control your typing behavior by setting it to adjust or highlight incorrect texts.
- **Speech:** This is used to manage and improve speech settings whenever you notice a deficiency in your PC speech recognition.

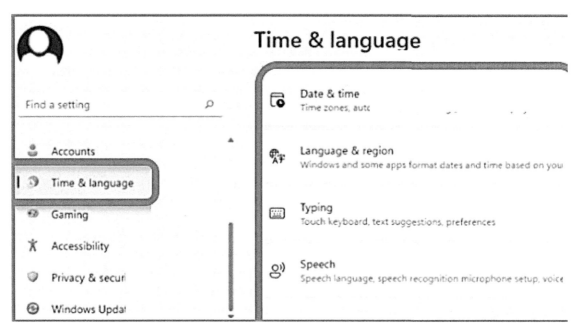

Gaming

This feature allows you to control the following sub-divisions;

1. Xbox game bar: This feature allows you to manage options relating to the Game Bar.

2. Captures: This feature allows you to select the location to save your images. You also get to choose options related to the following;

- Video quality
- Maximum Recording Duration
- Video Frame Rate

3. Game Mode: This feature allows you to activate the game mode of your device.

Accessibility

Accessibility is a feature that improves your access to and use of the internet. It makes computers work for people who have difficulty using computers. Accessibility helps people who have difficulties using their keyboard, voice, mouse, or other devices. Accessibility options change how a computer behaves and can also improve performance. They include:

- Mouse
- Speech
- Keyboard

These options are available for the Windows Operating System. It doesn't matter which OS you use to access the internet; these tools are available to improve your experience. Many people take these options for granted. They might not realize how much their own computer is changing.

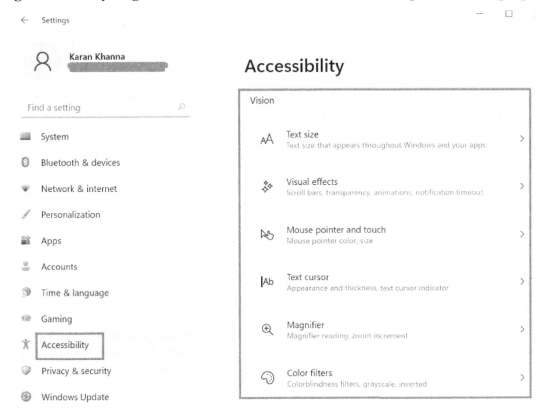

Accessibility options can have a significant impact on how you use your computer. You might feel frustrated if you're not sure how they work. Fortunately, they're pretty easy to set up and use if you're willing to look around.

This topic will help you get started using the mouse as a case study.

What is Mouse Accessibility?

A lot of people struggle to use their mouse. It's easy to imagine why. The mouse can be difficult to control. Some people even struggle to see their mouse or their mouse pointer. Some people have issues when they move the mouse. For example, they might see blurry images or have trouble moving the mouse to the right location.

You can make the mouse work better if you have any of these issues. You can make your mouse easier to see. You can make it work better for people with eye or vision problems. Check out the mouse accessibility options in Settings and some helpful troubleshooting tips.

Right-click

Right-clicking is a mouse accessibility feature that's relatively easy to set up and use. The right-click option gives you a couple of extra mouse clicks on your operating system's desktop. You can right-click to open up new programs, save documents, and share files.

You can right-click a mouse pointer to open or move windows.

For people with vision problems, this can make it easy to right-click things and make them easier to use. It makes using the mouse easier, whether you're trying to open a window or save a document.

Dragging

Mouse accessibility options aren't limited to the right-click option. Dragging is another option that's really helpful for people who are using a mouse.

The mouse accessibility options in your operating system might help you drag around your desktop. You can open or close programs and move items around your desktop. You can save or share files with just a mouse drag and a simple click.

For people with vision problems, this makes dragging easier. You can drag programs or files around and open them with just a simple click. With mouse accessibility options, the drag-and-drop option works really well.

Toggle Buttons

One of the mouse accessibility features you might have missed is the ability to change how the mouse works on your computer. For example, you might be able to make the scroll wheel just a click instead of a drag.

You might have noticed this on your computer. With mouse accessibility features, you can change how the scroll wheel works on your mouse.

This option might be a great addition to your mouse for people with vision problems. You can change the default scroll wheel and make it click instead of drag. You can make it easier to move documents, programs, and files around.

Alternate Input Devices
Your computer might support more than just a mouse. Your mouse might not be the only input device. If you have an external mouse, then your computer might also support other input devices, such as a keyboard or trackball. Your computer might allow you to switch between devices as needed.

For people with vision problems, this option might work really well. It gives you access to all the input devices on your computer. You can use all the input devices your computer supports at any time.

Privacy & Security

This feature helps to solve issues related to the following fields;

1. <u>Security</u>: This particular feature controls the following sub-divisions;

- The health of your P.C.
- Virus and Threat protection
- Account Protection
- Firewall and Network protection
- App and Browser control
- Device security
- Device performance
- Health
- 'Find My Device' feature
- Advanced settings for developers.

2. <u>Windows Permission</u>: This feature controls the following subdivisions;

- General
- Speech
- Inking and Typing
- Personalization
- Diagnostics and Feedback
- Activity History
- Search Permissions
- Searching Windows
- Online Speech recognition
- Storage of the history of your online and offline activities
- Activation of Safe search
- Activation of Cloud Content Search
- The setting of Indexing options.

3. <u>App permissions</u>: This feature is what you should check when you need to activate or deactivate the app permissions of the following applications;

- Location
- Call History
- Notifications
- Calendar
- Account information
- Automatic File downloads
- Videos
- Pictures
- Microphone
- Voice Activation
- Contacts
- File System, etc.

Windows Update

This feature allows you to alter the settings regarding the newly uploaded updates of your P.C. You would be able to know the last time you ran an update on your device—the time and the date. You would also know when you are due to run another update on your device. The features below are a list of the other things you could do when you get to the Windows Update settings feature;

- You can temporarily stop an update from being installed on your computer
- You get to view the records of your previous updates
- You get to download updates over a metered connection
- You get to program your active hours
- You get to 'Buy Microsoft Office.'
- You get to access other updates
- You would find tabs needed for Advanced features
- The Windows Insider Program

Chapter 9:
Emailing With Family And Friends

The Windows Mail app allows you to receive and send out emails. When you log in on your Yahoo, Google, Windows Live, or AOL account, this app will automatically set up and sync your contacts with your **People** list.

The Windows 11 Mail App

Email has become essential to everyday life; Windows 10 accommodates this with the Mail App.

Click on the Mail app on the start menu, then click on the get started button. Click on add account, select the type of account you want to set up, enter your e-mail address and password and click sign in. Once connected, the account details are shown under the mail heading, including Mailboxes within the account. Click on the inbox to view the emails within it. An electronic address book is always a good feature to have on a computer, and with Windows 10 this function is provided by the People apps. This can be found on the start menu.

If you have ever used any other email client, the Mail app shouldn't be too difficult to get to grips with. The main interface is split into three main sections (from left to right): Navigation, Message List and Reading Pane.

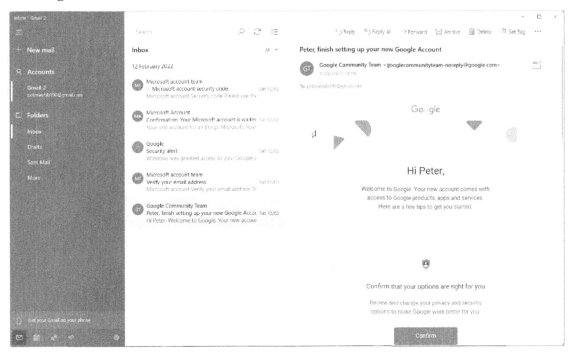

Navigation

The navigation sidebar on the left contains a list of your different email accounts and the different folders within those accounts (Inbox, Drafts, etc). At the bottom of the section are links to the Calendar, People and To Do apps, as well as the Mail Settings.

Message List

Select any of the folders in any of your email accounts, and the messages will be displayed as a list in the middle section of the interface. At the top is a search field, so you can search for specific emails and controls to filter and sort your emails. Select any email in this section to open it in the Reading Pane section.

Reading Pane

The majority of the Mail app interface is reserved for displaying the email content when one is selected in the Message List. When an email is displayed here, a number of controls appear at the top, including Reply, Forward, Archive and Delete. Select the More button to see more options.

Setting Up A New Email Account

- Open the Mail app using the Start menu.
- Select Add account if you are using the app for the first time.
- If you have used the app before, you will need to go to Settings at the bottom of the navigation pane on the left, then select Manage Accounts.
- Choose what kind of account you would like to set up. You can choose to use an existing Outlook account or create a new one. You can also use an Office 365, Google, Yahoo, or iCloud account. Alternatively, you can use other types of email accounts that use POP or IMAP, but this will require advanced setup options.
- If you choose a Google account and have enabled two-step verification (recommended), you must enter your unique 2-step verification code sent to your email or phone number.
- Enter the information required for sign-in, including the email address and password.
- Select Done and your account will begin syncing. The mail app will download all of your email and contacts for you.

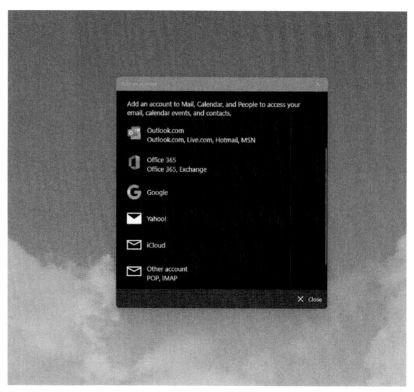

Advanced Setup

Older types of email accounts may require advanced setup options. Select Advanced options when prompted, and then input the necessary information.

Adding Multiple Email Accounts

If you have several Microsoft Accounts or a specialised work or school account, you are free to add all of your Microsoft Accounts to Windows, including their contact lists, emails, and calendar events. Return to **Accounts > Email & Accounts > Settings > Accounts > Email & Accounts**. Click the **Add a Microsoft account or Add a work or school account option** under the Accounts used by other applications section.

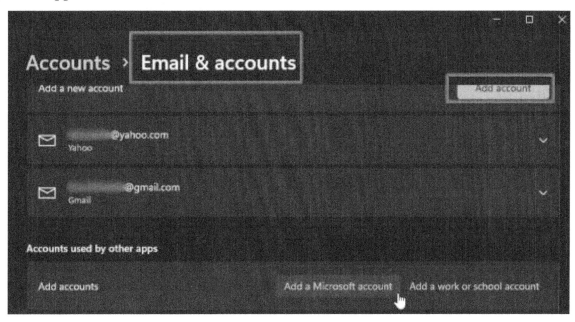

Enter your Microsoft Account, work account, or school account email and password in the Sign-in box. To sign in and verify the account, just follow the steps. The new account should now show up in the **Email & Accounts section**.

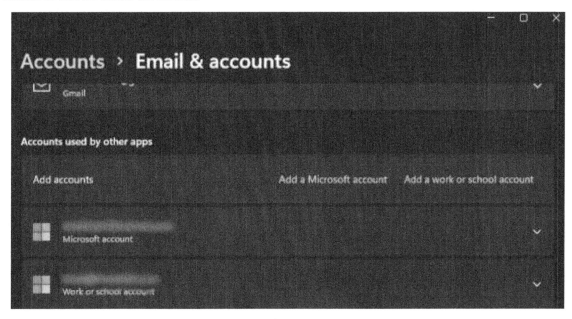

Inside the Mail app, you can now browse mail, contacts, and calendar events from your other Microsoft account and your work or school account. On the left, select **Accounts**, and then on the right, click **Add account**.

The newly added account should be at the top of the list. If not, choose the account type and input your email address; the account should appear. Click **Done** after selecting the account name. You can move on to access the account's email, calendar, and contacts using the Mail app.

Using The Mail App

You will see several buttons in the navigation pane on the left side of the Mail App.

- Collapse - collapses the navigation pane to reduce clutter.
- + New mail - compose a new email.
- Accounts - View your account information.
- Folders - includes your Inbox, Drafts, Sent, and Archive folders.
- Switch to Mail - Used to toggle between the Mail and Calendar apps.
- Switch to Calendar - used to toggle between the Mail and Calendar apps.
- Settings - access the Mail App settings.

You will see a search bar, a refresh button, and a selection mode button in the messaging list pane. You can use the search bar to look for specific terms or keywords in your emails. The refresh button will automatically download and upload all incoming and outgoing mails. The selection mode can select specific emails for the deletion or move them into a different folder. Finally, the reading/writing pane is on the right side of the window.

How To Compose An Email and Attach Files To An Email

Composing an Email
If you follow these steps, creating and sending a message is simple:

- Open the Mail program on your computer.
- Select the account you want to use to send a new email from the left pane.
- Click the **New mail icon** in the left pane.
- In the **"To" field**, type the recipient's email address. *Quick Tip:* If you use a semicolon to separate each address, you may send the same email to many people (;).
- In the **"Subject" field**, provide a title for the email.
- Click the message body button to start writing your email.

Your message now has a Format tab, which includes tools for formatting text, lists, and headers, as well as undo and redo options. Go to the **Insert tab** and choose **Files** from the Files drop-down menu if you want to send a file. This tab can also be used to share photos, links, and even tables.

You can send the message or discard it by selecting the Send button in the top-right corner.

Attaching Files

- In Windows Mail, create a new email message.
- From the drop-down option, choose Attach **File to Message**. (*The symbol you're searching for is the paperclip*.)
- In the Open dialogue box that appears, choose the file you want to attach, then click Open. Explore the folders in the Open dialogue box as you would in Windows Explorer.
- Type your e-mail message normally, but in the Attach text box, type the attached file's name.
- Press the **Send button** to send or transmit data.

How To Read And Reply To Emails

Email checking and response are identical to what you'd expect from a web browser or other client.

To see and respond to emails, use the techniques listed below:

- Open the Mail program on your computer.
- Select the account you wish to send a new email from the left pane.
- Go to the **"Folders" area** and find the email list.
- Choose the email you want to read from the message list, and it will appear in the right-hand reading window. If you need more space to read or compose emails, you can always collapse the left pane using the menu button in the top left corner.
- If the folder you need isn't shown, go to **More** and choose the folder you want to see, or right-click the folder you want and select **Add to Favorites** to have it appear under "Folders" all the time.
- Once in the email, you may use the reading pane toolbar to answer, forward the message to another person, archive, delete, or set a flag.
- By tapping the **menu (three-dotted) button** on the far left, you may access further options such as transferring the email to a different folder, designating it as spam, printing, and more.
- Use the search box above the message list window if you can't find the email you're searching for. You may also use the left-hand drop-down menu to categorize the list and search or manage your emails in several ways.

The Spam Folder

To access the junk or spam folder in the Windows 11 Mail app, follow the steps outlined below.

- In the Mail app's left-hand pane, select **More**. If you cannot see the **More option**, click on the three horizontal bars at the top to see the same.
- You should now get another pane with all your folders. Here, you should be able to see your spam or junk email folder.
- If you want to add the spam or junk folder to the left-pane of the Mail app, right-click on the spam or junk folder and click the **Add to favorites option**.
- You should now see the trash email or spam folder in the left pane of the Mail program.
- You can also right-click on the **garbage** or **spam** folder and choose **Pin to Start** to access the folder from the Start menu easily.

Creating Folders and Organizing Mail

Your mail will be sorted into different folders by default. The primary folders include:

- Inbox - This is where all of your primary emails can be found.
- Drafts - this is where you can find emails that you have started writing but have not yet sent.

- Sent items - this is where you find any emails sent by you.
- Archive - this is where you can find archived items.
- Deleted Items - the Mail app will store deleted emails for a limited time so that you can restore them if need be.
- Junk Email - This is where your junk and spam emails are stored for a limited time.

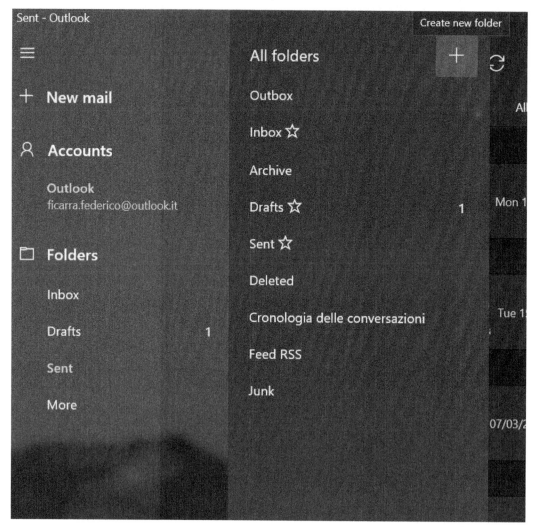

You can sort and organize your emails by creating more personalized folders such as Work, Personal, Friends, Family, etc. Right-click on the navigation pane to create a new folder and select "Create new folder." Also, you can create subfolders by clicking on an existing folder and selecting "Create new subfolder." For example, you may have a Work folder with subfolders such as Boss, Colleagues, Clients, etc.

You can arrange and sort your folders in order of importance by dragging and dropping them into place. You can also mark specific folders as Favorites by right-clicking and selecting "Add to Favorites." Your Favorite folders are pinned near the top of the Folders section in the navigation pane, so they are always easy to access, and you do not have to scroll to look for them.

Folders offer many other useful tools. Right-clicking on a folder allows you to rename, delete or move the folder to a new location. You can empty a folder or mark all the emails inside as read. Also, you can pin a folder to your Start menu, making it quick and easy to access your important emails.

Personalizing Your Mail App

Click the Settings button at the bottom of the Mail Navigation section, and click "Personalization" from the new open menu. Here, you can choose colors, light or dark mode, message spacing, and the app background image. All changes are displayed in the small preview at the top of the Personalization settings.

Google Mail

Google Mail is an excellent alternative to the Mail app; however, it can only be used with 'Gmail' email addresses.

- To use Google mail, visit www.gmail.com.
- Enter your Gmail email address & password to log in.

The Gmail web page has a similar layout to the Windows 11 Mail app, showing a navigation pane on the left where you can access all of your folders. You can also access Google Meet, a video conferencing service, and Google Hangouts, a cross-platform messaging service.

Your emails are shown in the central part of the web page. Unread emails and folders containing unread emails will be highlighted in bold. Click on the emails to view the whole message.

You can quickly sort through your emails using the checkboxes on the right of each mail, selecting or deselecting to delete, mark as read, or move emails to a different folder.

Composing an Email in Google Mail

1. To compose a new email, click the Compose button in the top left of the screen.

2. A small window will pop up at the bottom right of the screen. You can input your recipient's email address, CC or BCC other contacts, and define the subject line here.

3. The toolbar at the bottom of this window offers several features:

- Attach a file using File Explorer
- Insert a link
- Insert an emoji
- Insert a file using Google Drive
- Insert a photo
- Toggle confidential mode on or off
- Add a signature

4. To send a message, hit the Send button. By clicking the small arrow on the Send button, you can also choose to schedule a later time to send your message.

Google Mail Settings

The quick settings menu offers many options for personalizing the web page's appearance, including the layout, theme, inbox type and positioning of the reading pane. You can access more settings by clicking the "See all settings" button at the top of the quick settings. This will direct you to a new web page and here, you can access General, Labels, Inbox, Accounts and Import, Filters and Blocked addresses, Forwarding and POP/IMAP, Add-ons, Chat and Meet, Advanced, Offline and Theme settings.

Chapter 10:
Networking

Computer networks are everywhere these days, and everything seems to be connected to everything else, so it's important to know a little about basic networking to connect your computer other computers, wireless printers, etc. After all, the Internet is the world's biggest network, so without networking, we would all be just talking to ourselves... at least when it comes to our electronic gadgets.

Networking with Windows is not all that difficult if you just set up a basic home or small office network. When you start dealing with domains and multiple sites and networks connected, things get a little more interesting. But it's fairly easy to do if you just want to network a few computers together. I'm not going through a step-by-step demonstration because too many variables won't relate to your configuration, so I will just go over the basics.

Workgroups

Microsoft Teams is a good buddy if you are facing network issues and don't have enough capacity to make a great video or audio conversation. To experience high-quality video or voice with anybody outside or within your company, teams simply need a speed of about 1.2 Mbps.

This program helps users by allowing them to connect in groups of ten to ten thousand individuals regardless of where they are.

Small businesses with less than twenty workers utilize Skype. The software is free if you wish to purchase credit to initiate to mobile networks.

This business tool lets you host teleconferencing conversations for up to two hundred and fifty people, as well as handle employee identities and give enterprise-grade security.

Chat Functionality
The capabilities of the chat feature are one of the biggest distinctions between the two programs. In this regard, Microsoft Teams does have a significant edge over Skype. Users may be allowed access to any group or private and check its archives whenever they like with Microsoft Teams.

Besides those discussions that were erased singly and you can do absolutely nothing about, communications remain visible to you irrespective of the time you joined the chat.

The issue with Skype is subtly unique, but it is not to be faulted, although it's one of the best teleconferencing systems available. Chats aren't saved to your history after you have the window closed, but they do allow you the option of adding several connections to a chat group. There's a way to store chat chats, but you must utilize Outlook as your primary email program.

Transferring Files
Microsoft Teams allows you to exchange files even if they're not connected to the internet. You may transmit various assets, including GIFs, memes, and crucial documentation.

Because Skype doesn't provide an offline solution, you can only exchange files when online. You may, of course, specify file size limitations as well as the kind of items you'd like to transfer.

Guest Access

A guest in Microsoft Teams may start a channel or join a private conversation, exchange an item, and delete, edit, and post messages, which is advantageous over its larger cousin Skype.

Guests who do not yet have a registered Skype account must download the Skype application to attend a session on Skype. The invite is sent to them by calendar or email.

Domains

If you work at a company with a reasonable number of Windows computers, you are most likely part of a Windows domain. In a domain, all access and security are controlled by centralized servers called domain controllers. You log into your computer with your domain username and password, which determines your access to all network resources like file servers and printers. Using domains makes it easy for network administrators to control user accounts and permissions since it can all be done from one place and applied to the entire network.

To check your workgroup name or to see if you are a part of a domain, you can go to the *System* settings and then the *About* section. Then you will see a link that says Domain or workgroup, which you can then click on to take you to the screen as seen in the figure below. Next to the word Workgroup will be the workgroup name. (In my example, it's called WORKGROUP.) If your computer were joined to a domain, it would say *domain* rather than *Workgroup* in this section.

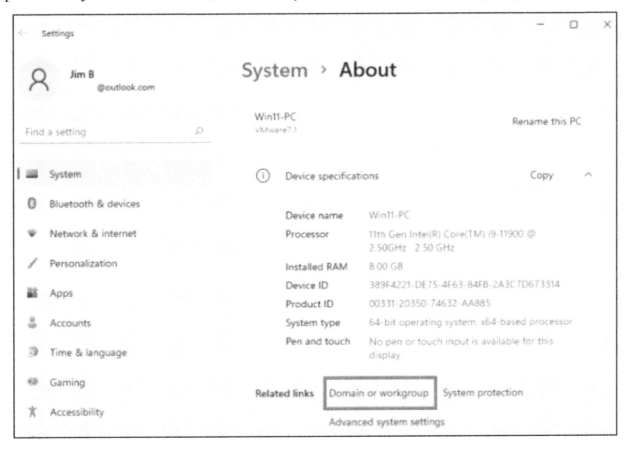

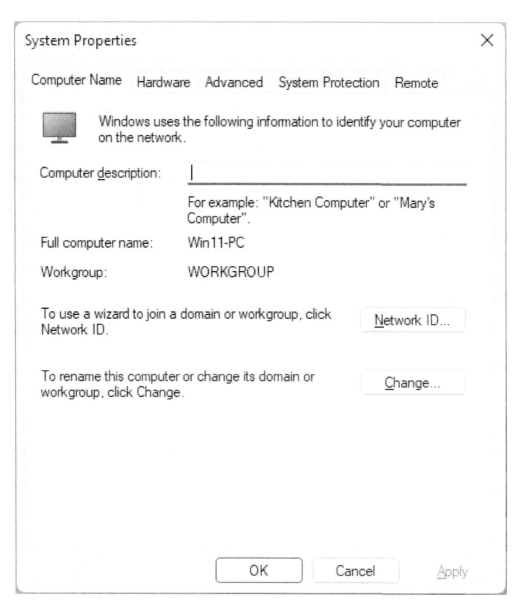

IP Addresses and Configuration

Using Settings

- Open Windows Settings

- Select Network & Internet

- Here, the network the PC is currently connected to can be seen.
- Click on Network and sharing center.
- Select Change adapter settings from the left menu.

- Right-click on the connected network and select Properties.

131

- On the next window, select Details.

The IPv4/IPv6 address can then be seen. This is the PC's current IP address.

Using Command Prompt
- Open Command Prompt
- Type in "ipconfig" and press Enter
- The result of this command shows a list of all current network adapters connected to the PC, including the Wi-Fi and Ethernet connections.

- Check through till a section labelled Ethernet adapter Ethernet" or "Wireless LAN adapter Wi-Fi" is located. There the PC's local IPv4 and IPv6 addresses can be seen.

Additionally, simply open to a web browser and searching "my IP address" would also give information on the system's IPv4 address.

Dynamic And Static IP Addresses

Another thing I want to mention about IP addresses is the difference between a static IP address and a dynamic IP address. Each one has its place in networking, so it's important to know the basic difference between the two. The address does not change when a device is assigned a static IP address. Nearly all devices use dynamic IP addresses given by the network when they connect and change over time.

DHCP

DHCP (Dynamic Host Configuration Protocol) simplifies the operation of IP address configuration by automating address configuration for network clients. For DHCP to work, it will require a device acting as a DCHP server. It can be a computer, router, or another type of network device.

Wireless Setup

With Windows 11 running on your device, you can connect to wireless networks effortlessly. And Windows 11 offers various means to connect to a wireless network.

One of the ways to manually set up wireless connections is via Settings app. If the network is in range or hiding its Service Set Identifier (SSID), the device can automatically connect to the network. To do this;

- Go to the Settings app.
- Then select the setting, **Network & internet.**
- Toggle **On Wi-Fi** and tap the option **Manage known networks** on the Wi-Fi interface.
- Click the link **Add network.**

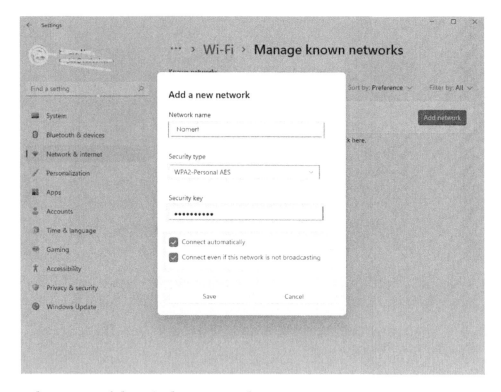

- Check out the name of the wireless network.
- Choose the Security type, WPA2-Personal AES via the drop-down menu on the Security type option.
- Enter the network password via the security key entry field and tick the options **Connect automatically** and **Connect even if this network is not broadcasting.**
- And then click on **Save** at the bottom of the window above.

Now, your device will automatically connect if the Wi-Fi network connection is in range as well as when it is visible or hidden.

Also, you can connect to a Wi-Fi network via the Taskbar with Windows 11 running in your device. And to do this;

- Toggle the **Network** icon at the bottom-right corner of the **Taskbar** to trigger the **Quick Settings.**

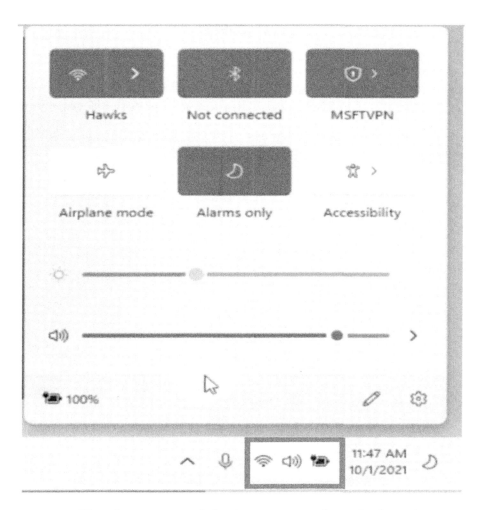

- Tap the **arrow right** icon next to the **wireless** icon.

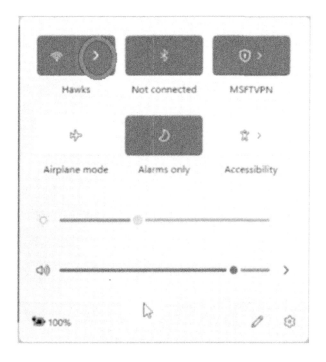

- Choose the wireless network connection and tick the option **Connect automatically** if you want.
- Then click on **Connect** to proceed.
- Enter the network connection password and tap **Next**.
- Check out if the computer is discoverable in the wireless network connection.

The device will now be connected to the wireless network. In addition, you can connect your device to a wireless network via the control panel and command prompt.

.

Chapter 11:
Having Fun with Windows 11

Since the release of Windows 11, the Photos app has been one of the most eagerly anticipated features. Several people can find a new Photos app uninteresting, but the new Windows 11 version has a distinctive style and some novel features that give it an advantage over the Windows 10 version. So, let's take a look at the picture app in Windows 11 and see how you can use it to view, edit, and improve your images.

Taking Photos And Videos

With Windows 11, you can easily take photos or videos and edit your media using some of Microsoft's default programs.

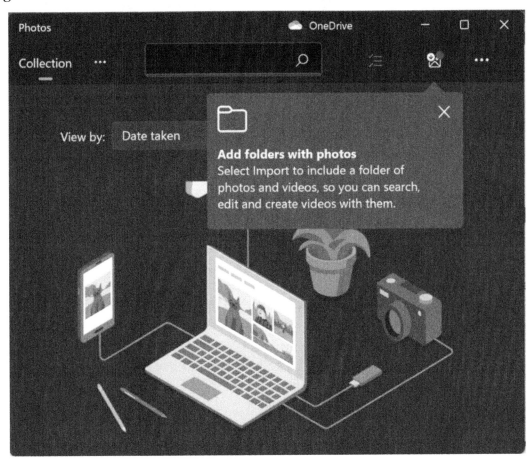

If you are using a Windows 11 laptop or mobile device like a tablet, it will likely come with a built-in camera that you can use to take pictures or videos.

1. Find out if you have a camera by typing 'Camera' into the Start menu.

2. If you see an icon appear, click on it to open the Camera app.

3. To use your camera, make sure it points towards the subject you want to capture in a photo or video. Check your screen to see a preview of the image and ensure everything is centered and framed correctly.

4. When you are ready, click the 'Capture' button on the left of the bottom of the screen.

5. First, click on the Video icon in the Camera app to take a video.

6. Press the 'Record' button to begin capturing footage, and then press the same button to stop recording when you are finished.

Viewing Your Photos and Videos

Windows 11 will save all the content you capture using your built-in camera to the "Camera Roll" folder in your Pictures Library. You can access this media using File Explorer.

Using the Photos App

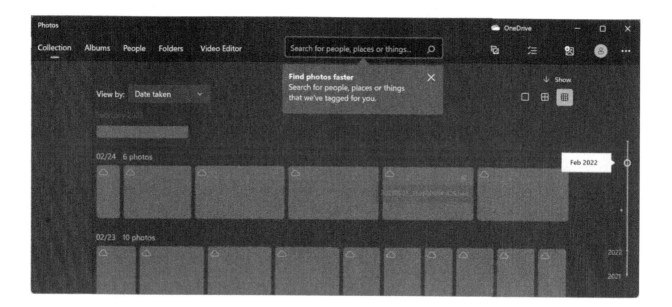

Viewing Details

- Each image or picture we view has a name and some information about it that we can't see. You may view their information in the Photos app.
- View an image in the Photos app by clicking on it. On the top of the picture, you'll see various controls. Then, on the right side, click the info icon to access a panel with the information about the selected image.

Editing Pictures

- When you view an image, you will notice various options, including the ability to alter it. To access editing options, click the edit button.
- Cropping, rotating, flipping, changing aspect ratios, adjusting brightness and contrast, and applying filters to photographs are all options on the editing screen. After making the necessary changes, click Save a copy to save the updated version.

Create an Album

- Clicking the double picture symbol in the Photos app's top bar to make an album. You will see options such as New video project, Automatic video, Backup import, and Album. Select Album.
- Then, tick the boxes in the corners of the photographs you wish to add to the album and click Create at the top of the Photos app.

Creating a Slideshow

- To view a slideshow of your photos in the Photos app, hit the three-dot button in the window's upper-right corner. Then, from the list of options, choose Slideshow.
- It will display a slideshow of all the photographs in the sequence in which they were taken.

Automatic Video

The Photos app has intelligent software that can curate your photos and videos and select a few to produce unique videos just for you.

- To create one of these automatic videos, click on the "New video" button on the right side of the toolbar and select "Automatic video."

Editing Videos

You can edit and even create videos using the new and improved Photos app in Windows 11.

1. Open the Photos app and click "Video editor" from the toolbar at the top of the window.

2. You will see a Project library on the left, a preview on the right, and a storyboard pane on the bottom.

3. Select the video or videos you want to include by pressing the 'Add' button in the Project library section.

4. A toolbar with several editing tools is at the top of the Storyboard pane. Click on the video you want to edit to use these tools:

5. You can add a title card to the beginning of your video.

6. Trim the length of the video.

7. Split the video into different sections.

8. Add text to the video.

9. Change the motion and positioning of the video.

10. Add 3D effects.

11. Add filters.

12. Change the speed.

13. Crop the video.

14. Undo the last action.

15. Delete this video from the project.

16. At the top of the Video editor window, you will see a pencil icon that you can use to rename your project. You can also add background music or custom audio from your File Explorer. You can also export the video in different formats by clicking "Finish video."

Facial Recognition

The Photos app can employ sophisticated facial recognition software to identify friends and family members in your photos and videos. You can use this feature to create collections of specific people.

1. Click on 'People' in the toolbar to turn on this feature. Click 'Yes' to allow facial recognition.

2. The feature will run in the background and create different groups based on the faces.

3. You can rename the groups to match the person's name by right-clicking the collection and selecting 'rename.'

Upload Images To The Photos App
- By default, the Photos app finds the photos on your computer. If you don't see any folders or photographs in the Photos app, you may quickly import them. Click the import button in the top bar of the Photos app and choose the option that best suits your needs. Images can be imported from a folder or a linked device.

Change An Image's Date
- The Photos app allows you to modify the date of a photograph simply. To alter the date, right-click on the image you wish to modify the date on and select Change Date. Then, from the context menu, choose Change date.
- It will display the dates. Adjust them as needed, then click the tick box to save the date.

Sort Photos By Persons
- The Photos app also has a function for effortlessly grouping photographs of a person. The People feature the one that organizes photographs of people by recognizing faces in each image. To arrange or group photos by person, go to the Photos app's top bar and select People.
- Turning on the People setting requires your consent. To activate it, kindly press the Yes button.
- The Photos app takes a few moments to read and recognize individuals in each image and group them.

Adding Favorites
- If you liked a few images in the collection and don't want to waste time looking for them again, you can save them to your favorites. By adding them to favorites, you may access them anytime by navigating to the favorites section of the Photos app.
- To add a photo to your favorites, click the heart icon at the top of the image you're looking at.
- Alternatively, you may right-click on a picture and choose to Add to favorites from the menu that appears.

Modify The Look Of The Photos App
- You may also adjust the appearance of the Photos app by selecting Light, Dark, or Use System Settings. To do so, tap the three-dot icon in the upper-right corner of the Photos app and then pick Settings.
- It will launch the Photos app's Settings. Scroll down to the Appearance section and select the checkbox next to the appearance you wish to use.

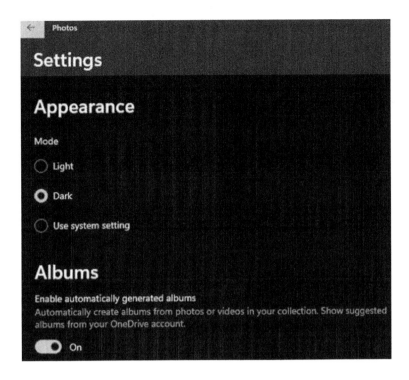

Scanning Photos And Documents

Many unique innovations and a new graphical interface are included in Windows 11, including a centered Start menu and taskbar, rounded edges windows, themes, and colors that make any Windows device stand out.

One thing you can do with Windows 11 is scan your papers and store them digitally anyplace using the built-in program. Users wishing to convert physical documents to digital formats and keep them on their computer, or the cloud may find installing a scanner is the best option.

Scanning App and Scanner

The easiest way to scan a photo or document using a scanner is with the Windows Scan app.

1. Download the Windows Scan app from the Microsoft Store.

2. Once the app is installed, open it up.

3. You will find some printer/scanner options, the file format you want your scan to be saved as, the color mode, page size, and which folder in which you would like the scan to be saved:

4. Some printers have feeders and flatbeds; many only have flatbeds. A scanner with a feeder can scan both sides of a page while you need to flip the page over when using a flatbed manually.

5. Hit the 'Scan' button at the bottom when you set all these options.

6. The scanner will import your file and save it in the specified location.

Microsoft Lens

Another way to scan content and save it onto your computer is to use the Microsoft Lens app. This is for mobile devices like smartphones and tablets that have cameras built-in.

1. Download Microsoft Lens from the Microsoft Store or Google Play Store. Ensure you download the correct app by checking that Microsoft Inc publishes it.

2. Once the app is downloaded onto your mobile device, open it up.

3. You may need to grant access to the app to use your camera and access your files and media.

4. The app will then open your camera.

5. Point it to the document or image you want to scan. When it is in the frame, hit the 'Capture' button.

6. The next step is properly adjusting the borders to fit the image or document's corners. You can drag the tabs shown to adjust these borders.

7. When you are done, hit the 'Confirm' button.

8. You will see a scan of your photo or document, and you can make adjustments using the options provided, such as crop or filters.

9. You can also add multiple pages or images using the 'Add' button.

10. When you have finished scanning, select the 'Done' button and input a name for the scan and the file format in which you want it to be saved. You can then pick a location where it will be saved.

11. If your mobile device runs Windows 11, the files will reflect what you can see on your PC. However, if you run on a different operating system like Android or iOS, you can select the scan and send it to your Microsoft email address, where it can be downloaded.

12. The Microsoft Lens app lets you choose what kind of media you want to scan and adjusts its settings to capture the highest quality image. You can select Actions, Document, Whiteboard, Business Card or Photo on the capture screen.

Native Games

Windows operating systems have a long history of including games in their products. Some of the most nostalgic titles include Minesweeper, Solitaire, 3D Pinball, and Hearts. Most of these games have been phased out, and Windows 11 is only compatible with the Solitaire Collection, which includes Classic Solitaire, Spider Solitaire, and FreeCell. These card games follow the same rules as their real-life namesakes.

To download and install the Solitaire Collection, open the Microsoft Store by clicking the app icon in your app list or type it into the Start menu. Search for the Solitaire Collection and click the Install button. You can launch the game by selecting Play.

Once the game runs, you can make it easier to access by pinning it to your taskbar or Start menu. Right-click on the game icon found on the toolbar and select "Pin to taskbar" or "Pin to Start."

Microsoft Store

On the desktop, an app store is a relatively new concept. However, it's something that Windows users have had for a while, and the Microsoft Store in Windows 11 makes it simple to search, compare, install, and update software.

Taking your initial steps in the Microsoft Store might be intimidating if you're accustomed to downloading software from websites and installing it using a setup application.

How to Access the Microsoft Store
You can visit the Microsoft Store either via the app that comes with Windows 11 or through the website.

The Microsoft Store should have a shortcut pinned to the taskbar (it looks like a shopping bag with a Microsoft logo), but it can also be found in the Start menu. Select the **Start button**, then either browse through the programs displayed or put Microsoft Store into the search box and click the shortcut that appears.

How to Check the Categories
Apps, Gaming, and Films and TV are the three primary divisions of the shop. The screen's button on the left-hand side may be used to access them. To begin, we'll look at applications.

There are many options for locating what you're searching for. If you know what you're looking for, put the name of an app into the Store's search box at the top and choose the appropriate item from the results. You may also go through the handpicked content categories, such as Best productivity apps, Best creative apps, and so on.

Choosing An App From The App Store
When you click on an app's name, you'll be transported to its listing page, where you can see images of the app in action, read the developer's description and user reviews, and learn more about the software's size and system requirements.

Installing applications, especially ones that are free, is a breeze. Simply click the **Get button** and wait for the program to download and install; a progress bar will appear as the download progresses.

The Get button becomes an Open button after the installation is complete. You may utilize the shortcut generated in the Start menu or click here to activate the program. Paid applications function similarly, but we'll return to them when we discuss payment choices.

Checking for available updates
It is critical to keep your applications up to date, whether free or paid. Installing the most recent version of a program gives you access to all of the newest features, as well as any bugs that have been detected.

Click the **Library icon** in the bottom left corner of the Store, then the Get updates button in the upper right corner to check if any updates are available.

It's also worth noting that many of the programs included with Windows 11 may be updated this way, so it's worth checking for updates regularly.

Clicking *the Context Menu*
You can also view a list of applications you've previously installed or installed on other devices when in the Library area. You can tell which ones are new by checking the button next to the applications you've previously loaded.

You'll see an **Open button** for applications you've installed, a button with a cloud, and a down arrow for apps you've already installed or loaded on other devices. You may download the app in question by clicking this button.

If you click the button, you'll be sent to a page where you will discover shortcuts for sharing the app through different channels and leaving a review if you'd like to share your thoughts with others.

Checking The App Settings
While the Microsoft Store is a rather straightforward program in and of itself, there are a few options you can tweak to make your life a bit simpler. Select **App settings** from your profile image in the top right corner of the app.

App updates are perhaps the most significant and helpful option here since if you allow it (by clicking the toggle to the right), any applications you have installed will be automatically updated, saving you from having to do it manually. It's still a good idea to check for updates on your own from time to time, just in case an essential update is provided outside of the normal timetable.

How To Add A Payment Method
You must have a method of payment linked with your account to install paid-for applications.

- To do so, go to your profile icon in the top right corner of the Store app and choose Payment methods from the drop-down menu. In your normal web browser, you'll be sent to your Microsoft account, where you'll be asked to check in using your password.
- Then, using the links provided, you may add a credit or debit card to your account and connect your PayPal account to utilize money from it to pay for Store content.

Using Payment Codes
The Microsoft Store, like many other software retailers, allows you to make purchases using gift cards and payment coupons. If you've received or purchased one of these, you can redeem it by choosing **Redeem code or gift cards** from the menu that shows when you click your profile icon in the top right corner of the Store window.

The related credit will be added to your account, ready to use, whether you manually input the 25-character code or use your camera to code it to save typing.

Purchasing TV series and films
The procedure of purchasing paid applications or games and purchasing or renting movies and TV episodes is remarkably similar to obtaining free material.

In the case of applications and games, after you've discovered anything you want, you'll be prompted to confirm the purchase by clicking the price button on the listing page.

It's the same thing when it comes to movies and television series. In many cases, you may choose from a variety of video quality choices, which can affect the amount you pay.

Managing the Store Account
Click your profile icon in the top right corner of the Store window and choose **Manage account** and devices to alter different settings associated with your Microsoft account.

You'll be brought to the Microsoft account page, just as when you add a payment method. You may alter your security settings and payment methods from here, as well as examine your purchase history and manage the devices and family members you've linked to your account.

How To Listen to Music

You can listen to music on your Windows 11 computer in so many ways. You can use streaming services like Spotify or use a media player to listen to CDs or mp3s already on your computer.

Music Streaming
Spotify

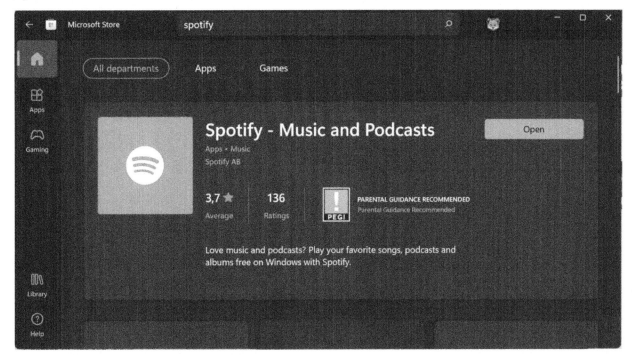

- You can download the Spotify application from the Microsoft Store.
- Once installed, open the app and begin the sign-in process by entering your password and email address, or you can sign up for a brand new account.
- You can sign in to the same Spotify account using multiple devices, allowing you to carry your music &playlists with you wherever you go.
- Navigate the Spotify app using the buttons down the left side:
- Browse - find new songs, artists, and genres to listen to
- Radio - allow Spotify to create a custom playlist based on a song, album, playlist, or artist that you have selected.
- Your Music - find your recently played songs, albums, artists, and stations that you have liked. You can also find Local files, where you can find downloaded content for listening offline.
- Playlists are where you can find your favorite playlists and Spotify's playlists that feature new music.
- In the middle part of the app, you can browse and discover new music or listen to your favorites. Use the search bar at the top to find specific tracks, artists, or albums.
- Use the player at the bottom of the app to pause, skip, adjust volume, and shuffle tings.
- Add friends who will appear on the right side of the app and see what they are listening to. You can share your music with your friends too.

Spotify Premium

The free version of Spotify grants you access to the entire music and podcast library, but you may be interrupted regularly by ads. The free version also prevents you from downloading content so that you can listen offline.

To take full advantage of the app's features, you will need to subscribe to Spotify Premium by following these steps:

- Visit www.Spotify.com and log in using your email address/username and password.
- Select 'Upgrade' in the menu bar.
- Select what kind of membership and price point you would like to pay for.
- Enter your payment information
- Refresh your desktop app, and you can now access Spotify Premium.

Groove Music and Windows Media Player

Both apps come standard with Windows 11 and can play most media files. You can use them to listen to music and create playlists. You can find either app by typing their name into the Start menu.

The main difference between the two is that Groove Music can be installed on multiple devices and will sync your songs, artists, albums, and playlists across these devices so that you can listen to your music wherever you go.

VLC Media

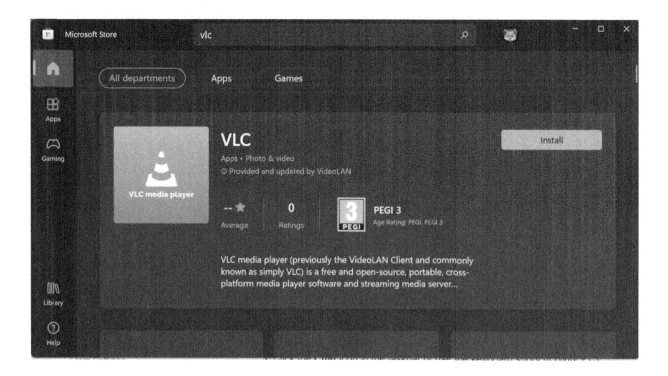

VLC is a third-party media player that can be used to view or listen to almost any kind of media file, including videos, music, podcasts, and more. It is a very simple to use and easy-to-understand app.

- To load media into VLC, find the content in File Explorer and drag it directly into the open VLC app window.

Chapter 12:
Tips, Tricks and Troubleshooting

Just like everything else in life, nothing works all the time perfectly, and that goes for computers and Windows as well. But if you learn some basic troubleshooting skills, you can fix many of the common problems you may encounter as you use your computer regularly.

Printer Troubleshooting

Strange Characters (Gibberish) appearing on the Page

Check your printer property settings under the Advanced tab to ensure the right driver is being used.

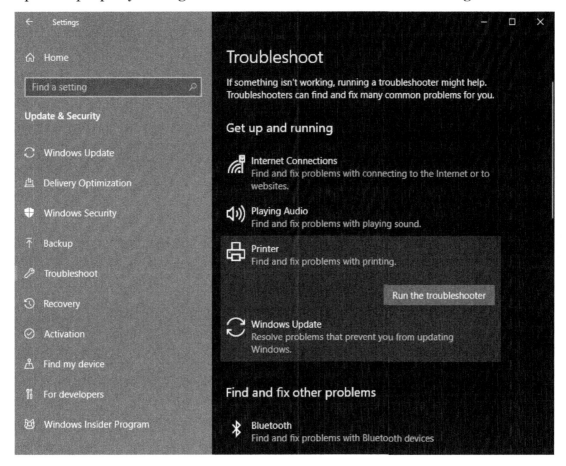

Wireless And Internet Troubleshooting

Sometimes, you might encounter problems with your Wi-Fi, which can be frustrating. To fix this problem;

- Go to settings.
- Click network & internet.
- Click on advanced network settings at the bottom of the page.
- Under more settings, click on network reset.

- On the next page, click on Reset now and confirm your action. Note that all Wi-Fi networks, including VPN networks will be deleted, so you might have to set them up again after this reset.
- Restart your PC and proceed to set up new networks.

It is important to note that this process might not solve your network problems if your access points are faulty or if there is an issue with your wireless adapter or driver.

Error Messages, Crashes, And Freezing Issues

Broken Apps

In case your apps are not working properly, especially the ones from Microsoft Store, Windows allows you to repair them. To do this, follow the steps provided below:

- Go to the **Start** button and click on the **Setting** icon
- Go to the **System** icon, click on **App** on the left-hand side, and **Apps and features** on the left-hand side.

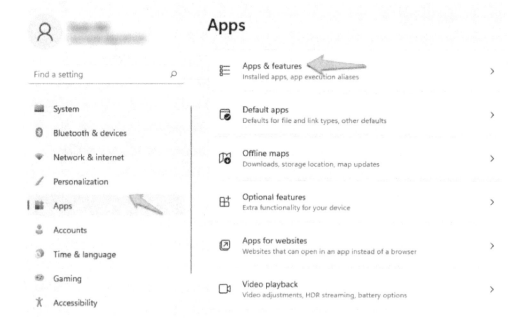

- Beside the name of the broken app, click on the **More** button. When the drop-down menu displays, click on the **Advanced options**

- In the **Advanced options** settings, click on the **Repair** button. If the Repair button cannot fix the broken app, click on the **Reset** button.

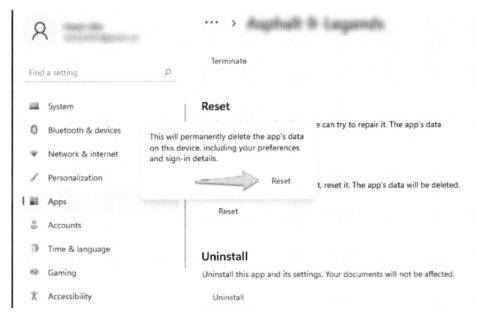

Desktop Keeps Crashing

If the RAM you installed and your storage devices conflict with Windows 11, the issue of Windows 11 keeps crashing can occur.

RAM

The function of the RAM on your computer is to save the temporary files of all of the installed programs on your and the various processes running on your PC. The desktop can crash quite easily if the system refuses to read them. This problem usually happens after installing additional RAM on your computer. Compatibility for Windows 11 cannot be relied on at this moment, so it is advised not to install an additional RAM.

Storage Devices

If you recently installed a new SSD, but it is damaged, the SSD can be the main cause of your Windows 11 keeps crashing and restarting. Try removing the SSD and check whether this problem persists or not. If the problem persists, then consider using some other alternatives that will be discussed below.

Second solution: Fix computer overheating

Computer overheating can cause a lot of issues for your computer. It can damage the hard drive or even crash your system. The Desktop keeps crashing issue in Windows 11 is also a very common challenge.

If your PC doesn't have a RAM and storage device issues but your desktop keeps crashing, try to shut down the system and let the computer rest.

Solution number three: Remove viruses and malware

Malware and viruses can equally cause the Windows crashing issue. Windows defender can be used to scan your computer for malware and viruses. In addition, you can try anti-virus software from third parties to scan and remove malware and viruses.

Solution number four (4): Update Device driver

Another common cause of Windows crashing is an outdated driver. This problem can simply be fixed when you update all devices' drivers. To do this, navigate to the **Settings,** select **Windows Update** and choose to **Check for updates** to see whether drivers updates are available. If yes, they can be installed automatically.

Solution number 5: Carry out an SFC scan

When your system files are missing, or they are corrupted, this can make the Windows 11 explorer.exe keep crashing and restarting. You can repair them by carrying out an SFC scan. Use the steps below to carry out an SFC scan in Windows 11;

- With the search space on the search bar, enter **cmd** to search.
- Select **Run as administrator**.
- You will be prompted with the **User Account Control** interface, and select **Yes** to continue.
- Type **scan /scannow** and click **Enter**. This tool will begin to run to search for corrupted or missing system files. The tool can repair them automatically, and you are expected to wait patiently.
- Restart your PC when the scanning ends.

Solution number 6: Fix the power issue

If it is your laptop you are using for Windows 11, the crashing desktop problem might be a result of a power issue. You can solve this problem by disabling Microsoft ACPI-Compliant Control Method Battery. To do this, follow the methods below;

- Right-click **Start**.
- Navigate to the **Device Manager,** click on **Batteries, right-click on Microsoft ACPI-Compliant Control Method Battery, and** choose **Disable**.
- Restart your system.

And lastly: Roll back to Windows 10

If no solutions discussed above work, it looks like the beta version of Windows 11 is not meant for your computer. You can consider going back to Windows 10. The official version of Windows 11 will come on board by October this year, and you can then install a more stable version of Windows 11.

Freezing

Sometimes, your PC may decide not to move no matter how you press the keyboard. When this happens, use any of the following methods:

- Press Esc twice.
- Concurrently press **Ctrl, Alt,** and **Delete**: The Task Manager appears listing the names of the apps currently running on the system. Click on the name of the apps that causes the system to misbehave, and then click on **End Task**.
- Restart the computer
- Hold the power button of the system for 5 seconds before it goes off

Error Types

You can receive numerous errors on your computer, making it even harder to narrow down the cause sometimes.

- *Application errors* – These can be caused by faulty software in regard to how it was created\programmed. They can also happen because of an unexplained glitch in the software, a compatibility error with other software, or with Windows itself.
- *System errors* – When you see these, you can assume it's related to a Windows problem, or maybe even a hardware or driver issue. Many times a reboot will clear up these types of errors.
- *Stop errors* are usually caused by faulty hardware such as bad RAM or a bad sector on your hard drive. When you see these errors, you usually look at the famous Blue Screen of Death message on your monitor.
- *POST errors* – POST (Power on Self-Test) errors can be caused by faulty hardware or BIOS\motherboard misconfigurations. You usually hear a beep sequence on boot up, and then you can research the beep pattern to help narrow down the problem.
- *Runtime errors* – These are usually caused by corrupt application executables or system files that cause certain programs to shut themselves down or are not even open. Sometimes they can even cause your computer to freeze up.

Windows Blue Screen of Death (BSOD)

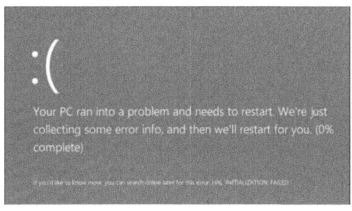

At times when you are running activity on your computer, you might suddenly see the screen turn blue, stopping all the activities and urging you to restart it. That is the Blue Screen of Death (BSoD). Its occurrence means that there was a very serious problem which has led to your computer system to crash.

Bluescreens occur due to some problems with the functioning of a computer's system. Here are some of the most common causes.

- Problems with an Operating System- Most bluescreens are experienced when there are problems with the Operating System. If the Operating System is not operating in a safe way, there are high chances of experiencing a system crash on your personal computer.
- Faulty hardware- If some of the hardware you use has a malfunction, a blue screen is sometimes experienced. It might result from a faulty memory, a hardware performing beyond its limits or even power problems causing overheating.
- Incompatibility- When your computer has some features that are not working in a proper way with others, there are chances of experiencing problems within the computer system. A system crash is imminent if the problem continues for some time.
- Malware/ Viruses- Another major contributor of Bluescreens is the presence of malware or viruses. These are harmful and can affect the running of your computer. You can experience duplication or deletion of your content or files. At times, the storage fills with nothing. The more they infect your computer, the higher the chances of getting bluescreens

How to Fix Bluescreens (BSoD)
Fixing a Blue Screen of Death requires time and may take up to several hours to completely fix. This depends on the STOP code, making the steps to solve the BSoD complicated or easy.

1. Reflecting on your Last Action

When it comes to the Blue Screen of Death, troubleshooting is made effective by taking note of the last action you had made or taken on your PC before the crash happened. In most cases, maybe it was after installing a new game, program or Windows update, making some updates for drivers or programs or introducing new hardware to the computer. Any of these pose a good chance for the occurrence of a BSoD.

In this instance, you can UNDO the change made and retest to ensure the STOP error is eliminated. In a bid to accomplish this, you can:

- Roll back the device driver to an earlier version before the driver update.
- Use the System Restore setting to undo recent system changes.
- Start up using 'Last Known Good Configuration' and undo the most recent driver and registry changes.

2. Do a Thorough Virus Scan

Viruses have been known to be the cause of the Blue Screen of Death from time to time. This is especially true for viruses infecting the boot sector or the Master Boot Record (MBR). To ensure this is effective, your antivirus must be up to date and configured to scan the boot and MBR sectors.

Finally, in some cases, you might not be able to access the antivirus on your Windows long enough to do the scan. In this case, you can use a Free Bootable Antivirus Tool or program as a replacement.

3. Create Space on your PC

Lack of space is probably one of the more common causes of the BSoD and other serious PC-related issues for example, data corruption. Therefore, you must ensure that your computer has adequate free space left on the drive on which your Windows is installed. This will solve the issues mentioned above as they come about when there is not enough space on the primary disk partition that facilitates all the operations of the Windows operating system.

It is advised that you always maintain not less than 100MB of free space, which can even be low for some machines. Therefore, the best case scenario is having at least 10%of the drive capacity free at all times.

4. Windows Updates and Maintenance

Having a Windows OS requires you also to take some time to update it and do maintenance actions as required. Information on how to do this is widely available online and on the Windows website. To be safe, you should regularly apply all available Windows service packs, patches, and updates. These keep you safe because they may contain bug fixes and other security features that address the causes of your BSoD.

5. System and Application Logs

Sometimes finding the cause of the bluescreen can prove to be a bit challenging. In such events, you can go into the application and system logs under Event Viewer to confirm if there are warnings or errors which may give a clue to the cause of the BSOD. There are plenty of online sources to guide you on how to start Event Viewer on your PC.

6. Hardware Drivers Updates

This should actually be one of the first actions you take after a BSoD. Take time to check for updates for all the drivers for the hardware on your computer. This is because a large percentage of bluescreen cases result from driver or hardware issues. Therefore, you can stop or fix the STOP error by simply updating the drivers.

7. Return Settings to Default

As mentioned above, most causes of BSoD are hardware related. Therefore, returning the hardware settings to default is a great solution! This can easily be done in the Device Manager. In fact, the system resources for individual hardware pieces should be configured for use in Device Manager and set to default to prevent the BSoD.

8. Update your BIOS.

This is as simple and straightforward as it sounds! Outdated BIOS can cause a Blue Screen of Death due to sets of resulting incompatibilities.

9. Check Installations

You have to make sure that cards, cables and any other components on your PC are properly placed and installed. In some instances, hardware that is not held firmly in position can cause bluescreens. You can do the following before retesting for the STOP error message:

- Check and fix any expansion cards
- Check and fix the memory modules
- Check and fix all internal data and power cables
- **Return BIOS settings to DEFAULT**

Another way to go about it is to return BIOS settings to their default levels. This is because misconfigured or overclocked BIOS may lead to multiple issues like Bluescreens. If you wish to maintain the customizations you had made, you can opt to return the voltage settings, BIOS memory and clock speed options to their default settings while testing to see if the STOP error is fixed.

10. Diagnostic Tests

As it has been established, hardware issues are some of the most prevalent when it comes to causes of bluescreens. Therefore, it makes a lot of sense to test all hardware by performing diagnostic tests to determine the root causes of the BSoD. This is usually a failing piece of hardware like the hard disk drive or system memory which must be tested.

Note: When either the hard drive or memory fails the diagnostic tests, replace them immediately!

11. Sticking to Essential Hardware

When starting your PC, ensure that only the essential hardware is connected to the computer. This is one of the most useful troubleshooting methods. Having only the minimum hardware necessary to run the operating system connected eliminates cases of BSoD. A successful start after this proves that one of the devices ejected was the cause of the STOP error.

Ideally, the necessary hardware to start a PC include the monitor, keyboard, video card, primary hard drive, CPU, RAM, and motherboard.

Using Task Manager And Ctrl-Alt-Del

The Task Manager shows each of the jobs (processes) as well as the machine's overall performance. The Task Manager may help you figure out how much memory a program is consuming, how to terminate a stuck application, and what system resources are available.

- **Press Ctrl + Shift + Escape**

In Windows 11, the tried-and-true Task Manager keyboard shortcut still works. To access Task Manager, just press **Ctrl + Shift+ Escape** on your keyboard.

- **Click the Start Button with your right mouse button**

If you'd prefer not to use the keyboard, right-click the Start button on your taskbar to open Task Manager. Select **"Task Manager"** from the menu that opens (commonly referred to as the **"power users menu"**).

- **Start a search in Start**

You can also search for **"task manager"** in the Start menu. The Task Manager app should come up first. To use it, just double-click its icon.

- **Use the Command Prompt**

```
Microsoft Windows [Version 10.0.22000.348]
(c) Microsoft Corporation. All rights reserved.

C:\Users\sysadmin>taskmgr
```

You can also use the Command Prompt to launch Task Manager. When the Command Prompt window appears, enter **taskmgr** on an empty line (for taskmgr.exe, the actual program's filename) and press **Enter**.

- **Make use of the Run Window**

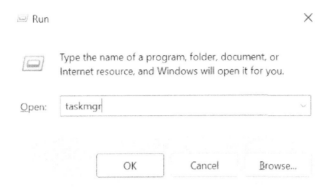

Task Manager may be launched from the Windows Run box, much as Command Prompt. To open the Run window, press **Windows + R, type taskmgr**, then click **"OK" or hit Enter**. The Task Manager will start up.

- **Hit Ctrl + Alt + Delete**

Finally, if none of the above methods worked, you may access Task Manager from the **Ctrl +Alt+ Delete** screen. You'll get a dark screen with a few choices in the middle after hitting **Ctrl+ Alt + Delete** on your keyboard. Task Manager will appear once you click **"Task Manager."**

System Configuration Utility (Msconfig)

The Windows System Configuration utility (also known as MSconfig since that's what most people type in the search or run box to open it) has been around for many years and is still a valuable tool for troubleshooting.

When you open the System Configuration utility, you will notice that it has several tabs just like Task Manager does. Once again, we will go over what each tab does so you can get an idea of how the System Configuration utility can help you manage and troubleshoot your computer. The easiest way to open this tool is to type **msconfig** in the search box.

General – Here, you can choose how you want your computer to start up regarding device drivers and services. *Normal* will load all drivers and services, *diagnostic* will load only the basic drivers and services, and *selective* will let you choose what services and startup items are loaded. The default is Normal, but the Normal startup option changes to Selective startup if you click any of the options in Advanced Troubleshooting Settings dialog box.

Boot – This tab lets you decide what operating system to load if you have more than one installed on your computer. The Boot options section lets you choose how your computer boots. So, if you want to do some diagnostics or testing, you can choose *Safe boot* and choose what options to load with it. The safe boot is the same thing as booting into Safe Mode, where you would press F8 on startup to load a basic configuration of Windows. Just be sure to change it back to normal after you are done so it won't go into Safe Mode on your next reboot. You can also change the timeout setting from the default of thirty seconds, so it will load the default operating system faster if you have more than one.

Services – Just like Task Manager, MSconfig has a Services tab, but here you can enable and disable services, so they start or don't start with Windows. This comes in handy for diagnosing issues, and if you have some services that don't need to start every time with Windows, you can disable them to improve your computer's performance. (Just be sure you know what the service does before enabling or disabling it.)

Startup – In older versions of Windows, this would be where you would see what programs are set to run when Windows starts, but in Windows 10 it just shows a link to open Task Manager, which will take you to the Startup tab there. This is one of the most commonly used areas because it allows you to prevent software from starting up that doesn't need to run every time you boot your computer, saving you resources and also allowing the computer to start faster. Virus and spyware infections love to put items in your startup section so they will load every time you start your computer. So, if you are having a virus or spyware issue, this should be one of the first places you check to see if there is anything set to run that shouldn't be running, and then you can disable it.

Tools – This tab will let you run a variety of common tools all from one location. Some of these tools include Task Manager, System Restore, and Event Viewer. You can open all these tools from their default location, but it's nice to see them all in one place. Plus, you may even discover a tool you didn't know existed.

Booting With The Windows DVD To Run Repair Utilities

BIOS (Basic Input and Output System) in a computer is the set of instructions it's microchip uses when booting after switching on the computer. It additionally manages data communication between the computer's OS and connected hardware devices such as hard disc, keyboard, mouse, etc.

Accessing BIOS through Settings
- Open Settings
- Select System

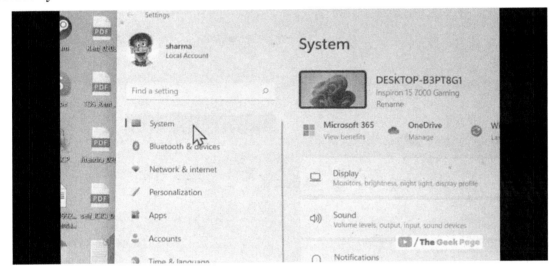

- Click on Recovery and then scroll down to Recovery options.
- Select Advanced setup option and click on Restart now button on the side.

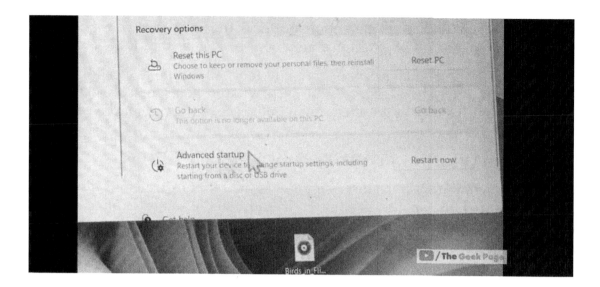

- On restart, select Troubleshoot from the Choose an option menu.

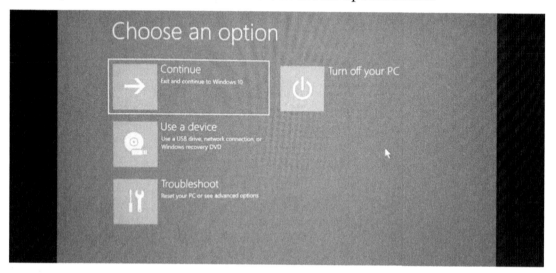

- Select "Advanced options" and then UEFI Firmware Settings.

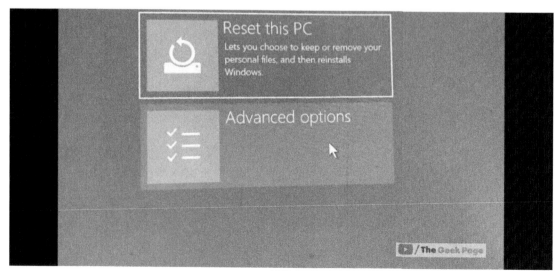

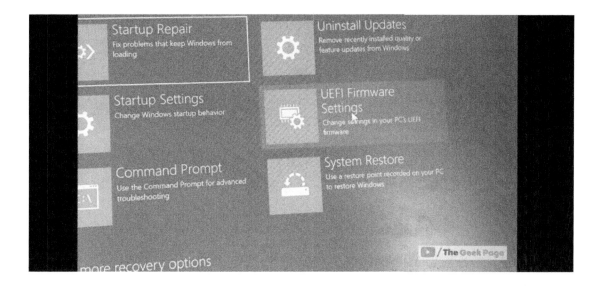

- Click on Restart;

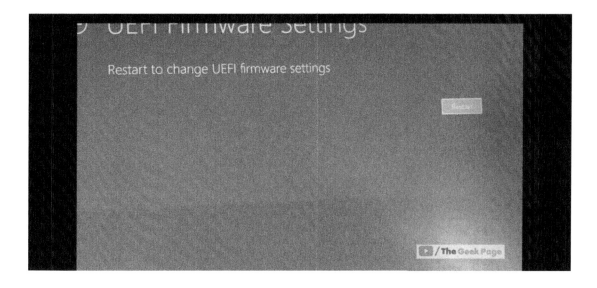

On restart, the computer routes to its UEFI/BIOS page.

Accessing BIOS using Shift + Restart

This can be done wherever the power button is visible, either on the lock screen, sign-in page, or the Start menu itself.

- Simply press down the Shift key on the keyboard and click Restart
- On restart, follow through with previous steps in the "Choose an option" menu.

Accessing BIOS from the Run Window

- Open Run using Window key + R
- Type in "shutdown /r /o /f /t oo" and click OK or press Enter
- The computer then notifies it is about to restart. On restart, it displays the "Choose an option" menu.

The same process goes for if the Windows terminal, Command Prompt or PowerShell is to be used.

- Launch the said applications and enter the command "shutdown /r /o /f /t 00" then press Enter.

The PC restarts and the options menu is displayed.

Conclusion

Windows 11 comes with a whole lot of new features that aid users in productivity, creativity, and gaming experience. It allows you to connect to people you care about faster and get the best apps through the newly designed Microsoft Store.

This guide, Windows 11 Manual contains everything there is to know about Microsoft Store, including Navigating through File Explorer, how to manage the settings, how to create a local or Microsoft account, how to project to a wireless display, how to boot into safe mode, how desktop works and so much more.

Reading through this guide has given you a grip on downloading, installing, and using Windows 11 on your PC.

Thank you for reading!

Printed in Great Britain
by Amazon

11888566R00093